10/00

D0777167

 St. Louis Community College

Forest Park
Florissant Valley
Meramec

Instructional Resources
St. Louis, Missouri

GAYLORD S

The
WISDOM
of
JESUS

O<small>THER</small> <small>TITLES IN THIS SERIES</small>

The Wisdom of Hinduism, ISBN 1–85168–227–9
The Wisdom of Buddhism, ISBN 1–85168–226–0
The Wisdom of the Qur'an, ISBN 1–85168–224–4
The Wisdom of the Tao, ISBN 1–85168–232–5
The Wisdom of Judaism, ISBN 1–85168–228–7

R<small>ELATED TITLES PUBLISHED BY</small> O<small>NEWORLD</small>

God's BIG Book of Virtues
God's BIG Handbook for the Soul
God's BIG Instruction Book
The Oneworld Book of Prayer
Words to Comfort, Words to Heal

The
WISDOM
of
JESUS

Compiled by Geoffrey Parrinder

ONE WORLD

OXFORD

THE WISDOM OF JESUS
Oneworld Publications
(Sales and Editorial)
185 Banbury Road
Oxford OX2 7AR
England

http://www.oneworld-publications.com

Oneworld Publications
(US Marketing Office)
160 N Washington St.
4th Floor, Boston
MA 02114
USA

© Geoffrey Parrinder 2000

ISBN 1–85168–225–2

Cover design by Design Deluxe
Typeset by Cyclops Media Productions
Printed and bound by Graphicom Srl, Vicenza, Italy

CONTENTS

PREFACE

JESUS WAS one of the great storytellers of the world. Many of his teachings are known in every Christian community and far beyond. Such stories as the Prodigal Son, the Good Samaritan, the Rich Man and Lazarus, and many others are universal and timeless. His wisdom was taken from the common things of life, daily and homely themes, illustrated in ways that all can understand.

The wisdom of Jesus is not speculative philosophy. There is no debate about the existence of God, which is taken for granted. Rather it is the nature of God and his relationship with humanity that matter. God is called Father, a merciful and loving parent who cares for every creature. In the marketplace, two sparrows cost a farthing, and when five are sold for two farthings, the worthless make-weight is known to the heavenly Father.

More debatable was belief in life after death, denied by the priestly Sadducees. On this matter, Jesus sided with the Pharisees and argued his faith in a future life from the Law itself, the Torah, the most sacred scripture. The Pharisees were a devout party, who later guided Judaism through the crisis of the Roman destruction of the Temple in Jerusalem in 70 CE. They appear in the Gospels as puritanical, with the virtues and limitations of puritans, and their opposition to the later breakaway Christian movement is reflected in some of the texts.

The wisdom of Jesus is seen in his actions, and indeed his person, as well as in his words, so making a selection and fair presentation difficult: this book is not the story of his life. Yet his life is often tied up with the sayings, and although some stories stand on their own, others are better understood against their background, or reflect faith in the person as well as in the words. This is especially true at the end, in the narratives of the trial, crucifixion and resurrection, to which all the evangelists give considerable space. With no change of tone, the words of Jesus are delivered in very different circumstances. We have made selections from the accounts of those final days, to indicate important sayings among the narratives.

The accepted records of the words and works of Jesus are in the written Gospels, and they are remarkable in themselves. An eminent Jewish scholar, Geza Vermes, has emphasized the importance of the Gospels as historical narratives.

> Where the life story of Jesus is concerned, for instance, no serious scholar of today would query the main threads of the narrative: Jesus entered into his public ministry during the mission of repentance preached by John the Baptist; he enjoyed a greater measure of

success in Galilee; he clashed with the authorities in Jerusalem; he died there on a cross; and all this took place during the middle years of the prefecture of Pontius Pilate, who governed Judaea between A.D. 26 and 36.

The Gospel of Jesus the Jew, 1981, pp. 4–5

Professor Vermes goes on to discuss the relationship of doctrine to history in the Gospels.

If the evangelists were primarily preoccupied with teaching Christian doctrine, how are we to explain their choice of biography as their medium? They cannot have been influenced by tradition; no Jewish convention exists that the sayings of the sages should be transmitted in this way.

The importance of the life of Jesus to the early Christians is evident. He lived, taught, died and rose again. These elements have always been essential to Christian faith.

If the evangelists chose to tell the story of Jesus' life, it was because, whatever else they may have intended, they wished also to recount history, however unprofessionally. And if they included circumstances which were doctrinally embarrassing, it was because they were genuinely believed to be part of the narrative.

There came to be many attempts at relating the words and works of Jesus. Some attempts were fanciful and dubbed 'apocryphal' (hidden) but four Gospels became 'canonical', meaning accepted as authoritative by the Church. It seems that the first Christian preachers related the words and deeds of Jesus to suit their message, and such oral teaching lasted until the martyrdoms of Peter and Paul in Rome about 64 CE. Then, it is said, Mark, who had been a disciple and interpreter of Peter, 'wrote down carefully, but not in order, all that he remembered of the Lord's sayings'. Mark wrote about the time of the fall of Jerusalem, which is perhaps reflected in his chapter 13 about signs of the times.

It was also said that Matthew compiled sayings of Jesus in Aramaic or Hebrew. Since our Gospel of Matthew is written in Greek it is possible that the gospel combined the life-story given by Mark with words of Jesus taken from a document called Q (from German Quelle, source), which contained sayings of Jesus and was used by the authors of the Gospels of Matthew and Luke. These first three written Gospels are usually called Synoptic, because they give over all accounts of the works and teachings of Jesus; Matthew and Luke are often dated about 80–85 CE. Finally came the Gospel of John, very different from the Synoptics, with long discourses which seem to present reflections of the evangelist himself.

For the sayings of Jesus selected in this book, Matthew has been invaluable because of his groupings of words for teaching purposes, for example the Sermon on the Mount, chapters 5–7, or the long chapter 13 on parables. Luke is parallel, but different in many details.

As Jesus' ministry moved forward from teachings and healings in Galilee to the Passover pilgrimage and activities in Jerusalem in the last week of his life, so the application of the wisdom of Jesus progressed. His sayings noted the signs of the times and anticipated the destruction of the Holy City with warnings and judgement, before moving on to his own death. How much the records read back from what happened, it is impossible to say, but the agony in the garden and the silences of the trial show Jesus practising his own teachings of turning the other cheek, not resisting evil, and accepting the divine will. The cry of despair on the cross echoed countless human tragedies.

His kingdom and his wisdom seemed doomed to failure, but all the records recount an amazing recovery through resurrection appearances. These events are detailed in the four Gospels, Acts, and Paul's epistles. Paul claimed to have seen the risen Christ himself (1 Corinthians 9:1 and 15:8), and he quoted earlier, similar sightings by the disciples: by Peter, James the brother of Jesus, all the apostles, and many others.

Similar visions were claimed by Mary Magdalene, by Cleopas and his companion at Emmaus, and by the disciples in the upper room, at Bethany, at the lake, and on a mountain in Galilee. However these visions may be interpreted, the experiences changed the fugitive disciples into preachers with confidence and courage. The Wisdom that appeared defeated on Good Friday was transformed into success at Pentecost with three thousand followers (Acts 2:41). The words recorded of the risen Christ in differing contexts were reproduced by the Gospel writers in matter-of-fact ways: they are taken from church memories, like the whole story of Jesus's life and teachings.

This *Wisdom of Jesus* is not only of personal morality, it is concerned with society and justice. Running through the sayings, from first to last, is the ideal of the imminent Kingdom of God. The early church applied these teachings to Christian communities and society at large. With this faith the Roman empire was conquered, without a battle, when Christianity was chosen as the state religion by the emperor Theodosius in 380 CE.

This selection of sayings of Jesus is based on the translation of the Authorized, or King James, version, because it is traditional and written in the most memorable English. Many wonderful phrases that have nourished life and faith and literature for over four hundred years are in danger of being lost, if they are not preserved. Many young people nowadays may not be able to place or remember words such as: 'consider the lilies of the field', or 'blessed are the peacemakers', or 'let not your heart be troubled'. These sayings, and countless others, originated with the great translator William Tyndale in his New Testament of 1526, eighty per cent of his version being taken over by the Authorized Version in 1611. Of course there are archaic expressions and words, such as 'ye' or 'willeth', which can easily be modernized, and some revision has been followed in this book with reference to later translations.

GEOFFREY PARRINDER

THE DIVINE RULE

THE KINGDOM OF GOD

JESUS CAME into Galilee, preaching the Gospel of the Kingdom of God, and saying, The time is fulfilled, and the Kingdom of God is at hand: repent, and believe the good news.

MARK 1:14–15

AND GREAT multitudes were gathered together unto him, and he spoke many things to them in parables, saying, Behold, a sower went forth to sow; and when he sowed, some seeds fell by the wayside, and the birds came and devoured them:

Some fell upon stony places, where they had not much earth: and forthwith they sprang up, because they had no deepness of earth: and when the sun was up, they were scorched; and because they had no root, they withered away.

And some fell among thorns; and the thorns sprang up, and choked them.

But others fell into good ground, and brought forth fruit, some a hundredfold, some sixtyfold, some thirtyfold.

He that has ears to hear, let him hear.

Hear therefore the parable of the sower:

When anyone hears the word of the Kingdom, and understands it not, then comes the wicked one, and catches away that which was sown in his heart. This is he that received seed by the wayside.

But he that received the seed into stony places, the same is he that hears the word, and anon with joy receives it: yet he has no root in himself, but endures for a while: but when tribulation or persecution arise because of the word, by and by he is offended.

He also that received seed among the thorns is he that hears the word; and the cares of this world, and the deceitfulness of riches, choke the word, and he becomes unfruitful.

But he that received seed into the good ground is he that hears the word, and understands it; who also bears fruit, and brings forth, some a hundredfold, some sixty, some thirty.

MATTHEW 13:2–9; 18–23

PARABLES OF THE KINGDOM

THE KINGDOM of Heaven is like a man who sowed good seed in his field, but while men slept, his enemy came and sowed weeds among the wheat and went away. So when the shoots sprang up and bore fruit, then the weeds appeared also. And the servants of the householder came and said, Sir, did you not sow good seed in your field? How then has it weeds? He said, An enemy has done this. The servants said, Shall we go and gather them? But he said, No, lest in gathering up the weeds, you pull the wheat up with them. Let both grow together until the harvest and then I will tell the reapers, Gather the weeds first together, and bind them in bundles to be burnt; but gather the wheat into my barn.

The Kingdom of Heaven is like a grain of mustard seed, which a man took and sowed in his field; which indeed is the least of all seeds, but when it is grown, it is the greatest among herbs, and becomes a tree, so that the birds of the air come and lodge in its branches.

The Kingdom of Heaven is like leaven, which a woman took, and hid in three measures of meal, till the whole was leavened.

The Kingdom of Heaven is like treasure hidden in a field; which when a man has found it, he hides it, and for joy thereof he goes and sells all that he has, and buys that field.

Again, the Kingdom of Heaven is like a merchant, seeking goodly pearls; who, when he had found one pearl of great price, went and sold all that he had and bought it.

Again, the Kingdom of Heaven is like a net, which was cast into the sea and gathered fish of every kind. When it was full they drew it to the shore, and sat down, and they put the good into vessels, but cast the bad away.

Therefore every scribe who is instructed into the Kingdom of Heaven is like a man that is a householder, who brings forth out of his treasure things new and old.

MATTHEW 13:24–52

BEING ASKED when the Kingdom of God should come, Jesus answered, The Kingdom of God comes not with observation. Neither shall they say, Lo here! or, Lo there! for, behold, the Kingdom of God is within you.

LUKE 17:20–21

THE SERMON ON THE MOUNT – RELIGIOUS AND MORAL TEACHINGS

BEATITUDES – THE TRULY BLEST

SEEING THE multitudes Jesus went up into a mountain, and when he had sat down his disciples came to him, and he opened his mouth and taught them, saying:

Blessed are the poor in spirit: for theirs is the Kingdom of Heaven.

Blessed are they that mourn: for they shall be comforted.

Blessed are the meek: for they shall inherit the earth.

Blessed are they that hunger and thirst after righteousness: for they shall be fulfilled.

Blessed are the merciful: for they shall obtain mercy.

Blessed are the pure in heart: for they shall see God.

Blessed are the peacemakers: for they shall be called the children of God.

Blessed are they that are persecuted for righteousness' sake: for theirs is the Kingdom of Heaven.

Blessed are you, when men shall revile you, and persecute you, and say all manner of evil against you falsely, for my sake.

Rejoice, and be exceedingly glad: for great is your reward in heaven: for so persecuted they the prophets which were before you.

You are the salt of the earth: but if the salt has lost its savour, wherewith shall it be salted? It is thenceforth good for nothing, but to be cast out, and trodden under foot by men.

You are the light of the world. A city that is set on a hill cannot be hid. Neither do men light a lamp and put it under a bowl, but on a stand, and it gives light to all that are in the house.

Let your light so shine before men, that they may see your good works, and glorify your Father who is in heaven.

MATTHEW 5:1–16

BLESSED ARE you poor: for yours is the Kingdom of God.
Blessed are you that hunger now: for you shall be filled.
Blessed are you that weep now: for you shall laugh.
Blessed are you when men hate you, and when they keep you
out and revile you, and ban your name as evil for the sake
of the Son of Man.
Rejoice and leap for joy in that day; for your reward is great in
heaven, for so their fathers did to the prophets.

LUKE 6:20–23

THE GOLDEN RULE

ALL THINGS whatsoever you would that men should do to you, do even so to them: for this is the law and the prophets.

MATTHEW 7:12

AS YOU would that men should do to you, do also to them likewise. For if you love those who love you, what credit is that to you? For even sinners love those who love them.

And if you do good to those who do good to you, what credit is that? For even sinners do the same.

And if you lend to those of whom you hope to receive, what credit is that to you? For sinners lend to sinners, to receive as much again. But love your enemies, and do good, and lend, hoping for nothing in return, and your reward will be great, and you will be children of the Most High; for he is kind to the unthankful and evil. Be therefore merciful, even as your Father is merciful.

LUKE 6:31–36

MORALITY – LOVE YOUR ENEMIES

YOU HAVE heard that it was said by those of old time, Thou shalt not kill; and whosoever shall kill shall be in danger of the judgement:

But I say to you, That whosoever is angry with his brother without a cause, shall be in danger of the judgement.

Therefore if you bring your gift to the altar, and there remember that your brother has anything against you, leave there your gift before the altar, and go your way. First be reconciled to your brother, and then come and offer your gift.

MATTHEW 5:21–24

YOU HAVE heard that it has been said,
An eye for an eye, and a tooth for a tooth.
But I say to you, Resist not him that is evil,
> but whosoever shall smite you on the right cheek,
> turn to him the other also.
And if any one will sue you at the law, and take away your coat,
> let him have your cloak also.
And whosoever shall compel you to go one mile, go with him two.
Give to him that asks of you,
> and from him that would borrow from you, turn not away.
You have heard that it has been said,
You shall love your neighbour, and hate your enemy.
But I say to you, Love your enemies, bless those that curse you,
> do good to those that hate you, and pray for those who
> despitefully use you, and persecute you.
That you may be the children of your Father who is in heaven:
> for he makes his sun to rise on the evil and on the good,
> and sends rain on the just and on the unjust.
Therefore you must be perfect, as your heavenly Father is
> perfect.

MATTHEW 5:38–48

MORALITY – ADULTERY AND DIVORCE

YOU HAVE heard that it was said,
Thou shalt not commit adultery.
But I say to you, That whoever looks on a woman to lust after
    her has committed adultery with her already in his heart.
If your right eye offends you, pluck it out and cast it from you;
For it is profitable for you that one of your members should
    perish,
And not that your whole body should go to hell.

It has been said, Whosoever shall put away his wife,
Let him give her a writing of divorcement.
But I say to you, that whosoever shall put away his wife,
Except for the cause of fornication, causes her to commit
    adultery;
And whosoever shall marry her that is divorced, commits
    adultery.

MATTHEW 5:27–32

SOME PHARISEES came to test him, saying, Is it lawful to divorce one's wife for any cause?

He answered, Have you not read that he who made them from the beginning made them male and female? For this cause a man shall leave his father and mother, and shall cleave to his wife: and the two shall become one flesh. Therefore they are no more two, but one flesh. What therefore God has joined together, let not man put asunder.

They said, Why then did Moses command to give a writing of divorcement and to put her away?

He said, Because of the hardness of your hearts, Moses allowed you to put away your wives; but it was not so from the beginning.

And I say unto you, Whosoever puts away his wife, except for unchastity, and marries another, commits adultery.

His disciples said, If that is so, of a man with his wife, it is better not to marry.

He replied, Not everyone can receive this saying, but only those to whom it is given.

There are some eunuchs, who were born thus from their mother's womb; and there are some eunuchs, who were made eunuchs by men; and there are some eunuchs, who made themselves eunuchs for the sake of the Kingdom of Heaven.

He who is able to receive this, let him receive it.

MATTHEW 19:3–12

PRAYER

WHEN YOU pray, you must not be like the hypocrites: for they love to pray standing in the synagogues, and at the corners of the streets, that they may be seen by men.

Verily, I say to you, They have received their reward. But you, when you pray, enter into your inner chamber, and when you have shut the door, pray to your Father who is in secret; and your Father who sees in secret will reward you.

And when you pray, use not vain repetitions, as the heathen do: for they think that they will be heard for their much speaking. Therefore, do not be like them.

For your Father knows what things you need, before you ask him.

MATTHEW 6:5–8

ASK, AND it shall be given you;
Seek, and you shall find;
Knock, and it shall be opened to you.
For everyone that asks, receives,
And he that seeks, finds,
And to him that knocks, it shall be opened.
For what man is there of you, whom if his son asks for bread,
Will he give him a stone?
Or if he asks for a fish,
Will he give him a serpent?
If you then, who are evil, know how to give good gifts
     to your children,
How much more shall your Father who is in heaven
     give good things to those who ask him?

MATTHEW 7:7–11

PERSISTENT PRAYER

E TOLD them a parable to show that they ought always to pray and not to faint; saying, In a city there was a judge who did not fear God or regard man, and there was a widow in that city who came to him saying, Support me against my adversary.

And he would not for a while, but afterwards he said to himself, Though I do not fear God, nor regard man, yet because this widow troubles me, I will support her, lest she wears me out by continually coming.

And the Lord said, Hear what the unjust judge says. And shall God not deliver his own elect, who cry to him day and night, though he delays long over them? I tell you that he will deliver them speedily. Nevertheless, when the Son of Man comes, will he find faith on the earth?

LUKE 18:1–8

WHICH OF you who has a friend will go to him at midnight and say to him, Friend, lend me three loaves, for a friend of mine has come to me from a journey, and I have nothing to set before him?

And he will answer from within and say, Do not trouble me: the door is shut, and my children are with me in bed; I cannot rise and give you anything.

I tell you, Though he will not rise and give him anything, even though he is his friend, yet because of his importunity he will rise and give him as much as he needs.

And I tell you, Ask, and it shall be given you; seek, and you shall find; knock and it shall be opened to you.

LUKE 11:5–9

HAVE FAITH in God. Verily, I tell you, Whoever shall say to this mountain, Be taken up, and cast into the sea; and shall not doubt in his heart, but believe that what he says shall come to pass, he shall have it. Therefore I tell you, whatsoever things you pray and ask for, believe that you have received them and you will have them.

And when you stand praying, forgive, if you have anything against anyone, that your Father also who is in heaven may forgive you your trespasses.

MARK 11:22–25

THE LORD'S PRAYER

PRAY THEREFORE after this manner:
Our Father, who art in heaven,
Hallowed be thy name.
Thy kingdom come.
Thy will be done, on earth, as it is in heaven.
Give us this day our daily bread.
And forgive us our debts, as we forgive our debtors.
And lead us not into temptation, but deliver us from evil.

For if you forgive men their trespasses, your heavenly Father
    will also forgive you.
But if you do not forgive men their trespasses, neither will your
    Father forgive your trespasses.

MATTHEW 6:9–15

TWO MEN AT PRAYER

J ESUS SPOKE this parable to some who trusted in themselves that they were righteous, and despised others:

Two men went up into the temple to pray, one was a Pharisee, and the other a publican. The Pharisee stood and prayed thus with himself: God, I thank thee that I am not like other men, extortioners, unjust, adulterers, or even like this publican. I fast twice a week, I give tithes of all that I possess.

But the publican, standing far off, would not even lift up his eyes to heaven, but smote his breast, saying, God, be merciful to me a sinner. I tell you, this man went down to his house justified rather than the other: for every one that exalts himself shall be humbled, but he that humbles himself shall be exalted.

LUKE 18:9–14

ON ALMSGIVING

TAKE CARE not to practise your piety before men, to be seen by them, otherwise you will have no reward from your Father who is in heaven. Therefore, when you give alms do not sound a trumpet before you, as the hypocrites do in the synagogues and in the streets, that they may have glory from men. Verily, I tell you, they have their reward. But when you give alms, let not your left hand know what your right hand is doing, that your alms may be in secret, and your Father, who sees in secret, will reward you.

MATTHEW 6:1–4

TRUE TREASURES

LAY NOT up for yourselves treasures on earth, where moth and rust corrupt, and where thieves break through and steal. But lay up for yourselves treasures in heaven, where neither moth nor rust corrupt, and where thieves do not break through nor steal; For where your treasure is, there your heart will be also.

MATTHEW 6:19–21

ON SWEARING

GAIN, YOU have heard that it was said to them of old time, Thou shalt not swear falsely, but keep the oaths sworn to the Lord. But I tell you, Swear not at all, neither by heaven, for it is God's throne, nor by the earth, for it is his footstool, neither by Jerusalem, for it is the city of the great King. Neither shall you swear by your head, because you cannot make one hair white or black, But let your speech be, Yes, yes; or No, no, for whatever is more than these comes from evil.

MATTHEW 5:33–37

ON FASTING

WHEN YOU fast, be not of a sad countenance, like the hypocrites, for they disfigure their faces that they may appear to men to fast. Verily, I tell you, they have their reward. But you, when you fast, anoint your head and wash your face, so that you do not appear to men to fast but to your Father who is in secret, and your Father, who sees in secret, shall reward you.

MATTHEW 6:16–18

THEN THE disciples of John the Baptist came to him saying, Why do we and the Pharisees fast, but your disciples do not fast? And Jesus said, Can the wedding guests mourn, as long as the bridegroom is with them? But the days will come, when the bridegroom will be taken away from them, and then they will fast. No one puts a piece of new cloth on an old garment, for that which is put in tears away from the garment, and the rent is made worse. Neither do they put new wine into old wine-skins, else the skins burst and the wine is spilled. But they put new wine into fresh wine-skins, and both are preserved.

MATTHEW 9:14–17

FULFILLING THE LAW

D O NOT think that I have come to abolish the law or the prophets: I have not come to abolish but to fulfil them. For verily I say to you, till heaven and earth pass away, one iota or one dot shall not pass from the law till all is fulfilled.

Therefore whosoever shall break one of the least of these commandments, and shall teach men so, shall be called least in the Kingdom of Heaven. But whoever shall do and teach them, shall be called great in the Kingdom of Heaven.

MATTHEW 5:17–19

ON ANXIETY

NO ONE can serve two masters: for either he will hate the one and love the other; or else he will hold to the one and despise the other. You cannot serve God and Mammon.

Therefore I tell you, be not anxious for your life, what you shall eat, or what you shall drink; nor yet for your body, what you shall put on. Is not life more than food, and the body than raiment? Behold the birds of the air: for they sow not, neither do they reap, nor gather into barns; yet your heavenly Father feeds them. Are you not much better than they?

Which of you by being anxious can add a foot to his height? And why are you anxious about clothing? Consider the lilies of the field, how they grow; they toil not, neither do they spin: Yet I say unto you, That even Solomon in all his glory was not arrayed like one of these. Wherefore, if God so clothes the grass of the field, which today is, and tomorrow is cast into the oven, shall he not much more clothe you, O you of little faith?

Therefore, be not anxious, saying, What shall we eat? or, What shall we drink? Or with what shall we be clothed? For the heathen seek after all these things, but your heavenly Father knows that you need all these things. But seek first the Kingdom of God, and his righteousness, and all these things shall be added unto you. Therefore, be not anxious for the morrow, for tomorrow will be anxious for itself. Sufficient unto the day is the evil thereof.

MATTHEW 6:24–34

HEARERS AND DOERS

J UDGE NOT, that you be not judged. For with what judgement you judge, you shall be judged; and with what measure you give, it shall be measured to you. And why behold the speck that is in your brother's eye but do not consider the beam that is in your own eye? How will you say to your brother, Let me pull the speck out of your eye, and behold, a beam is in your own eye? You hypocrite, first pull the beam out of your own eye, and then you will see clearly to take the speck out of your brother's eye.

Enter in at the narrow gate. For wide is the gate and broad is the way that leads to destruction, and many go in by it. But small is the gate, and narrow is the way that leads to life, and there are few that find it.

Beware of false prophets, who come to you in sheep's clothing, but inwardly they are ravenous wolves. You shall know them by their fruits. Do men gather grapes from thorns, or figs from thistles? So, every good tree brings forth good fruit, and a bad tree bears evil fruit.

Not everyone who says to me, Lord, Lord, shall enter the Kingdom of Heaven, but he that does the will of my Father who is in heaven. Many will say to me on that day, Lord, Lord, have we not prophesied in your name, and in your name cast out demons, and in your name done many wonderful works? And then I will declare to them, I never knew you, depart from me, you evildoers.

Therefore, whosoever hears these words of mine, and does them, will be like a wise man, who built his house upon a rock: and the rain descended, and the floods came, and the winds blew, and beat upon that house, and it did not fall, for it was founded on a rock.

And everyone that hears these words of mine, and does them not, will be like a foolish man, who built his house upon the sand: and the rain descended, and the floods came, and the winds blew, and beat upon that house, and it fell. And great was the fall of it.

MATTHEW 7:1–5,13–27

WIDENING APPEALS

THE CENTURION'S SERVANT

WHEN JESUS had ended all these sayings in the ears of the people he entered Capernaum, and a certain centurion's servant, who was dear to him, was ill and ready to die. And when he heard of Jesus, he sent some Jewish elders beseeching him to come and heal his servant. And when they came to Jesus they besought him earnestly, saying, He is worthy that you should do this for him, for he loves our nation and built our synagogue. Then Jesus went with them, and when he was not far from the house the centurion sent friends to him, saying; Lord, do not trouble yourself, for I am not worthy that you should enter under my roof, and I did not think myself worthy to come to you. But speak the word only, and my servant shall be healed. For I also am a man set under authority, with soldiers under me, and I say to one, Go, and he goes; and to another, Come, and he comes; and to my servant, Do this, and he does it.

When Jesus heard this, he marvelled, and said to those who followed him, I have not found such great faith, even in Israel. I tell you, that many shall come from the east and west, and shall sit down with Abraham, and Isaac, and Jacob, in the Kingdom of Heaven. And when those that were sent returned to the house, they found the servant whole that had been ill.

LUKE 7:1–10/MATTHEW 8:5–13

WOULD-BE FOLLOWERS

AS THEY went along the road a man said to Jesus, Lord, I will follow you wherever you go. But Jesus said, Foxes have holes, and birds of the air have nests; but the Son of Man has nowhere to lay his head.

And he said to another, Follow me. but he said, Lord, let me first go and bury my father. Then Jesus said, Let the dead bury their dead. But you go and preach the Kingdom of God.

And another also said, Lord, I will follow you; but let me first go to say farewell to those at my home. But Jesus said, No one who puts his hand to the plough and looks back, is fit for the Kingdom of God.

LUKE 9:57–62

SAMARITANS – GOD IS SPIRIT

HE CAME to a city of **Samaria**, and Jacob's well was there. Jesus therefore, being wearied by his journey, sat down by the well. It was about midday.

There came a woman of Samaria to draw water, and Jesus said to her, Give me a drink. The Samaritan woman said, How is it that you, a Jew, ask a drink of me, a Samaritan woman? (for Jews have no dealings with Samaritans). Jesus answered, If you knew the gift of God, and who it is that said to you, Give me a drink, you would have asked him, and he would have given you living water.

The woman said, Sir, I perceive that you are a prophet. Our fathers worshipped on this mountain; and you say that in Jerusalem is the place where people ought to worship.

Jesus said, Woman, believe me, the time is coming when neither on this mountain nor in Jerusalem will you worship the Father. You do not know what you worship: we know what we worship, for salvation is from the Jews. But the hour is coming, and is now, when the true worshippers will worship the Father in spirit and truth: for the Father seeks such ones to worship him. God is spirit, and those who worship him must worship in spirit and truth.

At this his disciples came, and they marvelled that he was talking with a woman, yet no one said, What do you want? or, Why are you talking with her? Then the woman left her waterpot and went into the city, and said to the people, Come and see a man who told me everything that I ever did. Can this be the Christ? Then they went out of the city and came to him.

Meanwhile the disciples prayed him, Master, eat. But he said to them, I have food to eat that you do not know of. So the disciples said to one another, Has anyone brought him food? Jesus said to them, My food is to do the will of him who sent me, and to accomplish his work. Do you not say, There are still four months, and then comes harvest? But I tell you, Lift up your eyes and look at the fields; they are already white for the harvest.

Many of the Samaritans of that city believed in him, because of the saying of the woman, He told me all that I ever did. And many more believed because of his own word.

JOHN 4:5–10; 19–24; 27–35; 39–41

THE SABBATH

JESUS WENT through the corn fields on the sabbath day, and as they went his disciples began to pluck the ears of corn. And the Pharisees said to him, Look, why are they doing what is not lawful on the sabbath? And he said to them, Have you never read what David did, when he was in need and was hungry, he and those that were with him? How he went into the house of God, when Abiathar was high priest, and he ate the shewbread, which it is only lawful for the priests to eat, and he gave it also to those who were with him?

And he said, The sabbath was made for man, and not man for the sabbath. So the Son of Man is lord even of the sabbath.

MARK 2:23–28

H E ENTERED the synagogue again, and there was a man there who had a withered hand. And they watched him, to see whether he would heal him on the sabbath, so that they might accuse him.

And he said to the man with the withered hand, Stand here. And he said to them, Is it lawful to do good on the sabbath, or to do harm? To save life, or to kill? But they held their peace.

And when he had looked round on them with anger, grieved at the hardness of their hearts, he said to the man, Stretch out your hand. And he stretched it out, and his hand was restored whole as the other.

MARK 3:1–5

THERE WAS a woman who had had a spirit of infirmity for eighteen years. She was bent together and could not lift herself up. And when Jesus saw her, he called her and said, Woman, you are loosed from your infirmity. And he laid his hands on her, and immediately she was made straight, and glorified God.

And the ruler of the synagogue was indignant that Jesus had healed on the sabbath, and he told the people, There are six days in which people ought to work. In those come to be healed, and not on the sabbath. But the Lord replied, You hypocrites, does not each of you loose his ox or his ass from the stall on the sabbath, and lead it away to water? And should not this woman, whom Satan has bound for eighteen years, be loosed from this bond on the sabbath?

LUKE 13:11–16

WHICH OF you who has an ass or an ox that has fallen into a well, will not immediately pull it out on a Sabbath day?

LUKE 14:5

CLEANLINESS – EVIL COMES FROM WITHIN

SOME OF his disciples ate with defiled, that is unwashed, hands. Then the Pharisees and scribes asked him, Why do your disciples not follow the tradition of the elders, but eat with unwashed hands?

He answered, Isaiah prophesied well of you hypocrites, as it is written, This people honours me with their lips, but their heart is far from me; they worship me in vain, teaching as doctrines the commandments of men. For you put aside the commandment of God, that you may keep your own tradition.

For Moses said, Honour your father and your mother; and, Whoever speaks evil of father or mother, let him surely die.

But you say, If a man says to his father or mother, Whatever you might gain from me is Corban (a gift to God), he is free, he is no more permitted to do anything for his father or mother. So the word of God is made void through your tradition, which you have delivered. And you do many similar things.

When he had called the people to him again he said, Listen, all of you, and understand. There is nothing outside a man, which can defile him by going into him. But the things which come out of him, they are the ones that defile him.

And when he had entered the house, away from the people, his disciples asked him about this saying.

And he said, Are you also without understanding? Do you not see that whatever enters a man from outside cannot defile him; because it does not enter his heart, but his stomach, and so passes on? (This he said, making all foods clean).

And he said, What comes out of a man is that which defiles him. For from within, from the human heart, come evil thoughts, fornication, theft, murder, adultery, coveting, wickedness, deceit, licentiousness, envy, slander, pride, foolishness. All these evil things come from within, and they defile a man.

MARK 7:2–13; 14–23

SEEKING THE LOST

FORGIVENESS

THEY BROUGHT to him a paralysed man, lying on a bed. And seeing their faith, Jesus said to the paralytic, Son, be of good cheer; your sins are forgiven. And some of the scribes said to themselves, This is blasphemy. But Jesus knowing their thoughts said, Why do you think evil in your hearts? Which is easier, to say, Your sins are forgiven, or to say, Arise and walk?

But that you may know that the Son of Man has power on earth to forgive sins, he said to the paralytic, Arise, take up your bed, and go to your house. And he arose and went home.

And when the multitudes saw it, they marvelled, and glorified God who had given such power to men.

MATTHEW 9:2–8/MARK 2:1–12

EATING WITH SINNERS

A s JESUS passed on from there, he saw a man named Matthew, sitting at the tax office. He said to him, Follow me, and he arose and followed him.

And as he sat at table in the house, many tax collectors and sinners came and sat down with him and his disciples. And when the Pharisees saw it, they said to his disciples, Why does your Master eat with publicans and sinners? But when Jesus heard that, he said to them, Those who are well do not need a physician, but those that are sick. But go and learn the meaning of the text, I require mercy, not sacrifice. For I have not come to call the righteous, but sinners to repentance.

MATTHEW 9:9–13

THE LOST SHEEP

THE PUBLICANS and sinners all drew near to hear him. And the Pharisees and scribes murmured, saying, This man receives sinners, and eats with them.

And he spoke this parable to them, saying, What man of you who has a hundred sheep, if he loses one of them, does not leave the ninety-nine in the wilderness, and go after that which is lost, until he finds it?

And when he has found it, he lays it on his shoulders, rejoicing. And when he comes home, he calls together his friends and neighbours, saying, Rejoice with me; for I have found my sheep which was lost. Even so, there shall be joy in heaven over one sinner that repents, more than over ninety-nine just persons, who need no repentance.

LUKE 15:1–7

THE LOST COIN

OR WHAT woman, who has ten pieces of silver, if she loses one piece, does not light a candle and sweep the house, and seek diligently until she finds it?

And when she has found it, she calls her friends and neighbours together, saying, Rejoice with me; for I have found the piece which I had lost. Even so, there is joy in the presence of the angels of God over one sinner that repents.

LUKE 15:8–10

TWO SONS

WHAT DO you think? A man had two sons, and he came to the first and said, Son, go and work today in my vineyard. And he answered, I will not. But afterwards he repented, and went.

And he came to the second, and said the same. And he answered, I will go, sir; but he did not go.

Which of the two did the will of his father? They said, The first. Jesus said to them, Verily I say to you, that the publicans and the harlots go into the Kingdom of God before you. For John came to you in the way of righteousness, and you did not believe him. But the publicans and harlots believed him. And even when you had seen it, you did not repent afterwards and believe him.

MATTHEW 21:28–32

PRODIGAL SON AND LOVING FATHER

A MAN HAD two sons: and the younger of them said to his father, Father, give me the share of goods that falls to me. And he divided his living between them. And not many days later the younger son gathered all together, and took his journey into a far country and there wasted his substance with riotous living. And when he had spent it all, there arose a mighty famine in that land; and he began to be in want. And he went and joined himself to a citizen of that country, and he sent him into his fields to feed pigs. And he would have liked to fill himself with the husks that the pigs were eating. And no one gave him anything. But when he came to his senses, he said, How many of my father's hired servants have bread enough and to spare, and here am I perishing with hunger! I will arise and go to my father and I will say to him, Father, I have sinned against heaven, and against you. I am no more worthy to be called your son. Make me like one of your hired servants.

And he arose and came to his father. But when he was still a long way off, his father saw him, and was moved with compassion, and he ran, and fell on his neck, and kissed him. And the son said, Father, I have sinned against heaven, and against you. I am no more worthy to be called your son. But the father told his servants, Bring out the best robe and put it on him. Put a ring on his hand, and shoes on his feet. And bring the fatted calf here and kill it, and let us eat and be merry. For this my son was dead, and is alive again. He was lost, and is found. And they began to be merry.

Now his elder son was in the field, and as he came near the house he heard music and dancing. And he called one of the servants and asked what this meant. And he said, Your brother has come, and your father has killed the fatted calf, because he has received him safe and sound. And he was angry, and would not go in. So his father came out, and entreated him. And he said to his father, Lo, these many years I have served you, and I never disobeyed your commandment. And yet you never gave me a kid, that I might make merry with my friends. But as soon as this your son has come, who has devoured your living with harlots, you have killed the fatted calf for him! And he answered, Son, you are always with me, and all that I have is yours. It was right that we should make merry and be glad. For this your brother was dead, and is alive again. He was lost, and is found.

LUKE 15:11–32

THE GOOD SHEPHERD

VERILY, VERILY, I say to you, He who does not enter the sheepfold by the door, but climbs up some other way, is a thief and a robber. But he who enters by the door is the shepherd of the sheep. The porter opens to him, and the sheep hear his voice. He calls his own sheep by name, and leads them out. When he has brought out all his own, he goes before them; and the sheep follow him, for they know his voice. They will not follow a stranger, but will flee from him, for they do not know the voice of strangers.

Jesus spoke this parable to them: but they did not understand what he was speaking to them.

Then Jesus said to them again, Verily, verily, I say to you, I am the door of the sheep. All who came before me were thieves and robbers, but the sheep did not listen to them. I am the door. If any one enters in by me he will be saved, and will go in and out and find pasture. The thief only comes to steal, and kill, and destroy. I came that they might have life, and have it abundantly.

I am the good shepherd: the good shepherd gives his life for the sheep. But he that is a hireling, and not the shepherd, who does not own the sheep, sees the wolf coming, and leaves the sheep, and flees, and the wolf catches them and scatters the sheep. He flees because he is a hireling and does not care for the sheep. I am the good shepherd, I know my own and am known by mine, as the Father knows me and I know the Father. And I lay down my life for the sheep.

And I have other sheep, which are not of this fold. I must bring them also, and they will hear my voice. There will be one flock, one shepherd.

JOHN 10:1–16

MISSION AND OPPOSITION

REJECTION AT NAZARETH

J ESUS CAME into his own country, and his disciples followed him. As his custom was, he went into the synagogue on the sabbath day, and stood up to read. And there was delivered to him the book of the prophet Isaiah. He opened the book and found the place where it was written:

> The Spirit of the Lord is upon me, because he has anointed me to preach good news to the poor, he has sent me to proclaim deliverance to the captives, and recovering of sight to the blind, to set at liberty those that are bruised, and to proclaim the acceptable year of the Lord.

He closed the book, and gave it back to the attendant, and sat down. And the eyes of all in the synagogue were fastened on him. And he began to say to them, Today this scripture is fulfilled in your ears. And all bore witness, and wondered at the gracious words which proceeded out of his mouth. And they said, Is not this the son of Joseph?

And he said to them, Doubtless you will quote this proverb to me, Physician, heal yourself. Whatever we have heard was done in Capernaum, do it here also in your own country.

And he said, Verily, I say to you, No prophet is accepted in his own country. I tell you truly, there were many widows in Israel in the days of Elijah, when heaven was shut up for three years and six months, and there came great famine throughout all the land; but Elijah was sent to none of them, except to a widow woman at Sarepta, in the land of Sidon. And there were many lepers in Israel in the time of Elisha the prophet, and none of them was cleansed except Naaman the Syrian.

And when they heard these things, all in the synagogue were filled with wrath, and they rose up and cast him out of the city, and led him to the brow of the hill on which their town was built, that they might throw him down headlong. But he passed through the midst of them and went his way.

MARK 6:1/LUKE 4:16–30

MISSION

JESUS CALLED twelve disciples and sent them out saying: As you go, preach, saying, The Kingdom of Heaven is at hand. Heal the sick, cleanse the lepers, raise the dead, cast out demons. Freely you have received, freely give. Provide neither gold, nor silver, nor copper in your purses, nor bag for your journey, neither two coats, nor shoes, nor staff: for the workman is worthy of his keep.

Into whatsoever city or town you shall enter, inquire who is worthy in it, and stay there till you leave. As you enter a house, salute it. And if the house is worthy, let your peace come upon it. But if it is not worthy, let your peace return to you. And whosoever shall not receive you, nor hear your words, when you leave that house or city, shake off the dust from your feet. Verily I tell you, it shall be more tolerable on the day of judgement for the land of Sodom and Gomorrah, than for that city.

Behold I send you out as sheep in the midst of wolves: therefore be wise as serpents, and harmless as doves. But beware of men: for they will deliver you up to councils, and scourge you in their synagogues. You will be brought before governors and kings, for my sake, to bear testimony before them and the Gentiles. But when they deliver you up, do not be anxious about how or what you shall speak. For it is not you that speak, but the Spirit of your Father speaking through you.

Brother will deliver up brother to death, and the father his child; and children will rise against parents, and cause them to be put to death. And you will be hated by everybody, for my name's sake. But he that endures to the end will be saved.

MATTHEW 10:1,7–22

PERSECUTION FOR THE SON OF MAN

WHEN THEY persecute you in this city, flee to the next. Verily I tell you, You will not have gone through the cities of Israel, before the Son of Man comes.

A disciple is not above his teacher, nor a servant above his master. It is enough for a disciple to be like his teacher, and a servant like his master. If they have called the master of the house Beelzebub, how much more will they call those of his household? Therefore, fear them not. For there is nothing covered, that shall not be revealed, or hidden, that shall not be known. What I tell you in darkness, speak it in the light: and what you hear in the ear, proclaim it on the housetops.

Fear not those who kill the body, but are not able to kill the soul; but rather fear him who is able to destroy both soul and body in hell. Are not two sparrows sold for a farthing? And not one of them falls to the ground without your Father's will. But the very hairs of your head are all numbered. Fear not therefore, you are of more value than many sparrows.

Therefore, whosoever shall confess me before men, I will confess him also before my Father who is in heaven. But whosoever shall deny me before men, I will also deny him before my Father who is in heaven.

MATTHEW 10:23–32

EVERYONE WHO speaks a word against the Son of Man, it shall be forgiven him; but to him that blasphemes against the Holy Spirit it shall not be forgiven.

LUKE 12:10

ARE NOT five sparrows sold for two farthings? And not one of them is forgotten before God.

LUKE 12:6

FAMILY OR FAITH

I CAME to cast fire upon the earth; and would that it were already
      kindled!
I have a baptism to be baptized with, and how I am constrained
      until it is accomplished!
Do you think that I have come to give peace on earth?
No, I tell you, but rather division.
For henceforth there shall be five divided in one house,
Three against two, and two against three.
They shall be divided: father against son, and son against
      father;
Mother against daughter, and daughter against her mother;
Mother-in-law against her daughter-in-law, and
      daughter-in-law against her mother-in-law.

LUKE 12:49–53

HE THAT loves father or mother more than me, is not worthy of
    me,
And he that loves son or daughter more than me, is not worthy
    of me.
And he that does not take his cross, and follow after me, is not
    worthy of me.
He that finds his life shall lose it,
And he that loses his life for my sake shall find it.

He that receives you, receives me,
And he that receives me, receives him that sent me.
He that receives a prophet, in the name of a prophet,
Shall receive a prophet's reward.
And he that receives a righteous man in the name of a righteous
    man,
Shall receive a righteous man's reward.

And whosoever shall give oneú of these little ones only a cup of
    cold water to drink, in the name of a disciple,
Verily I tell you, he shall surely not lose his reward.

MATTHEW 10:37–42

FEEDING THE FIVE THOUSAND

THE APOSTLES returned to Jesus, and told him all that they had done and what they had taught. And he said to them, Come away by yourselves to a desert place and rest a while. For there were many coming and going, and they had no leisure even to eat. And they went away by boat to a desert place by themselves.

But people saw them going, and many knew them, and they ran there on foot from all the towns, and got there ahead of them. And when Jesus landed he saw many people, and was moved with compassion towards them, because they were like sheep without a shepherd: and he began to teach them many things.

And when the day was far spent, his disciples came and said to him, This is a lonely place, and the time is late. Send the people away, that they may go into the country and villages round about and buy themselves something to eat.

He answered and said, You give them something to eat. They replied, Shall we go and buy two hundred pennyworth of bread and give it to them to eat?

He said to them, How many loaves have you? Go and see.

And when they knew they said, Five, and two fishes.

Then he commanded them all to sit down, by companies, on the green grass. And they sat down in groups, by hundreds and fifties.

And he took the five loaves and two fishes, and looking up to heaven he blessed and broke the loaves, and gave them to the disciples to set before the people, and he divided the two fishes among them all. And they all ate and were filled. And they took up twelve baskets full of the fragments and of the fishes. And those who ate the loaves were about five thousand men.

And he made the disciples get into the ship at once to go to Bethsaida on the other side, while he sent away the people. And when he had sent them away, he went up a mountain to pray.

MARK 6:30–46

WHEN JESUS perceived that they were about to come and take him by force, to make him a king, he withdrew into a mountain, by himself, alone.

JOHN 6:15

Feeding the Five Thousand ☙ 89

BREAD AND WATER OF LIFE

WHEN THE people found Jesus on the other side of the sea, they said to him, Rabbi, when did you come here?

Jesus answered, Verily, verily, I say to you, You seek me, not because you saw signs, but because you ate the loaves and were filled. Do not labour for food which perishes, but for food which endures to eternal life, which the Son of Man will give you, for God the Father has sealed him.

Then they said to him, what must we do, to do the works of God?

Jesus answered, This is the work of God, that you believe in him whom he has sent.

So they said to him, What sign do you show, that we may see and believe you. What work do you do? Our fathers ate manna in the wilderness; as it is written, He gave them bread from heaven to eat.

Then Jesus said to them, Verily, verily, I say to you, It was not Moses who gave you the bread from heaven. But my Father gives you the true bread from heaven. For the bread of God is that which comes down from heaven and gives life to the world.

Then they said to him, Lord, give us this bread always.

Jesus said to them, I am the bread of life: he who comes to me shall not hunger; and he who believes in me shall never thirst.

JOHN 6:25–35

ON THE last day, the great day of the feast, Jesus stood and cried, If anyone is thirsty, let him come to me and drink. He who believes in me, as the scripture has said, Out of his heart shall flow rivers of living water.

But this he spoke of the Spirit, which those who believed in him were to receive: for the Spirit had not yet been given, because Jesus was not yet glorified.

JOHN 7:37–39

THE SEVENTY – COME UNTO ME

JESUS APPOINTED seventy others, and sent them out two by two into every city and place where he himself would come.

He said to them, The harvest truly is great, but the labourers are few. Therefore pray the Lord of the harvest, that he would send forth labourers into his harvest.

The seventy returned with joy, saying, Lord, even the demons are subject to us through your name.

And he said to them, I beheld Satan fallen as lightning from heaven. Behold, I give you power to tread on serpents and scorpions, and over all the power of the enemy, and nothing at all shall hurt you. Nevertheless, do not rejoice that the spirits are subjected to you, but rather rejoice because your names are written in heaven.

And he said privately to his disciples, Blessed are the eyes which see the things that you see. For I tell you, that many prophets and kings desired to see the things which you see, and have not seen them, and to hear those things which you hear, and have not heard them.

LUKE 10:1–2, 17–20, 23–24

A T THAT time Jesus said, I thank thee, O Father, Lord of heaven and earth, because thou hast hidden these things from the wise and prudent, and hast revealed them to babes. Even so, Father, for so it seemed good in thy sight.

All things have been delivered to me by my Father; and no one knows the Son, except the Father. Nor does anyone know the Father, except the Son, and anyone to whoever the Son wishes to reveal him.

Come unto me, all who labour and are heavy laden, and I will give you rest. Take my yoke upon you, and learn from me. For I am meek and lowly in heart, and you shall find rest for your souls. For my yoke is easy, and my burden is light.

MATTHEW 11:25–30

JOHN THE BAPTIST – WISDOM JUSTIFIED

WHEN JOHN heard in prison the works of Christ, he sent two of his disciples, and said unto him, Are you he who is to come, or should we look for another?

Jesus answered, Go and tell John the things which you hear and see: the blind receive their sight, the lame walk, the lepers are cleansed, the deaf hear, the dead are raised up, and the poor have the gospel preached to them. And blessed is he who is not offended by me.

And as they went away, Jesus began to speak to the multitudes concerning John: What did you go out into the wilderness to see? A reed shaken by the wind? But what did you go out to see? A man clothed in soft raiment? Behold, those who wear soft clothing are in king's houses. But what did you go out to see? A prophet? Yes, I tell you, and more than a prophet. For this is he, of whom it is written, Behold, I send my messenger before your face, who shall prepare your way before you.

Verily I say unto you, among those born of women there has not arisen a greater than John the Baptist. Nevertheless, he who is least in the Kingdom of Heaven is greater than he.

And from the days of John the Baptist until now the Kingdom of Heaven suffers violence, and the violent take it by force. For all the prophets and the law prophesied until John. And if you are willing to accept it, this is Elijah who was to come. He that has ears to hear, let him hear.

To what shall I compare this generation?

It is like children sitting in the markets, and calling to their fellows and saying, We have piped to you, and you have not danced; we have mourned for you, and you have not lamented.

For John came neither eating nor drinking, and they said, He has a devil. The Son of Man came eating and drinking, and they say, Behold a gluttonous man, and a wine-bibber, a friend of publicans and sinners. But wisdom is justified by her works.

MATTHEW 11:2–19

SEEKING OTHERS

BEYOND ISRAEL

J ESUS WENT away to the region of Tyre and Sidon. And he entered a house and would not have any one know it, but he could not be hid. For immediately a woman, whose young daughter had an unclean spirit, heard of him and came and fell down at his feet. The woman was a Greek, a Syro-phoenician by birth, and she pleaded with him to cast the demon out of her daughter.

But Jesus said to her, Let the children first be fed. For it is not right to take the children's bread and throw it to the dogs. But she replied, Yes, Lord, but even the dogs under the table eat the children's crumbs.

Then he said to her, For this saying, go your way; the demon has left your daughter. And when she went home, she found the demon had gone and the daughter was lying on the bed.

MARK 7:24–30

I T CAME to pass, when the time drew near for him to be received up, that he set his face to go to Jerusalem. And he sent messengers before him who entered a village of the Samaritans, to make ready for him. But they would not receive him, because his face was set to go to Jerusalem.

And when his disciples James and John saw this they said, Lord, do you want us to call down fire from heaven, to consume them? But he turned and rebuked them (and he said, You do not know of what manner of spirit you are; for the Son of Man came not to destroy men's lives, but to save them).

And they went on to another village.

LUKE 9:51–56
(Bracketed verse from variant manuscripts)

SHE LOVED MUCH

ONE OF the Pharisees asked Jesus to eat with him, and he went into the Pharisee's house and sat at table. And behold, a woman in the city, who was a sinner, when she knew that Jesus sat at table in the Pharisee's house, she brought an alabaster box of ointment.

And she stood at his feet behind him weeping, and she began to wash his feet with tears, and wipe them with her hair, and she kissed his feet and anointed them with the ointment.

Now when the Pharisee saw this, he said to himself, If this man was a prophet he would have known who and what sort of woman this is that is touching him: for she is a sinner.

Jesus said to him, Simon, I have something to say to you.

And he said, Master, say on.

Jesus said, 'There was a creditor who had two debtors: one owed five hundred pounds and the other fifty. And when they had nothing to pay, he freely forgave them both. Tell me, therefore, which of them will love him most?'

Simon answered, I suppose that he to whom he forgave most.

And he said, You have judged rightly.

And he turned to the woman, and said to Simon, Do you see this woman? I entered your house, and you gave me no water for my feet. But she has washed my feet with tears, and wiped them with the hairs of her head.

You gave me no kiss: but since the time I came in this woman has not ceased to kiss my feet.

You did not anoint my head with oil: but this woman has anointed my feet with ointment.

Wherefore I tell you, her sins, which are many, are forgiven. For she loved much. But he to whom little is forgiven, loves little.

And he said to her, Your sins are forgiven.

And those that sat at table with him began to say among themselves, Who is this that even forgives sins?

But he said to the woman, Your faith has saved you; go in peace.

LUKE 7:36–50

WHO SHALL CAST THE FIRST STONE?

ARLY IN the morning Jesus came into the Temple and all the people came to him, and he sat down and taught them.

And the scribes and Pharisees brought to him a woman taken in adultery, and when they had set her in the midst, they said to him, Master, this woman was taken in adultery, in the very act. Now Moses in the law commanded us, that such people should be stoned. But what do you say?

This they said to test him, that they might have something of which to accuse him.

But Jesus stooped down, and wrote on the ground with his finger. So when they continued asking him, he lifted up himself and said to them, He that is without sin among you, let him cast the first stone at her. And again he stooped down and wrote on the ground.

And they, when they heard it, went out one by one, beginning from the eldest, even to the last. And Jesus was left alone, and the woman standing in the midst.

And Jesus lifted himself up, and said to her, Woman, where are they? Did no one condemn you?

She said, No one, Lord.

And Jesus said, Neither do I condemn you. Go, and sin no more.

JOHN 8:2–11

BORN AGAIN OF THE SPIRIT

THERE WAS a man of the Pharisees named Nicodemus, a ruler of the Jews. He came to Jesus by night and said to him, Rabbi, we know that you are a teacher come from God, for no one can do the signs that you do unless God is with him.

Jesus answered, Verily, verily, I tell you, Unless a man is born again, he cannot see the Kingdom of God.

Nicodemus said, How can a man be born when he is old? Can he enter a second time into his mother's womb, and be born?

Jesus answered, Verily, verily, I tell you, Unless one is born of water and the Spirit, he cannot enter the Kingdom of God. That which is born of the flesh is flesh, and that which is born of the Spirit is spirit. Do not marvel that I told you, You must be born again. The wind blows where it wills, and you hear the sound of it, but you cannot tell where it comes from or where it is going. So it is with everyone who is born of the Spirit.

Nicodemus said, How can this be?

Jesus replied, Are you a teacher of Israel, yet you do not understand this? Verily, verily, I tell you, We speak of what we know, and witness to what we have seen, yet you do not receive our witness. If I have told you earthly things, and you do not believe, how will you believe if I tell you of heavenly things?

JOHN 3:1–12

THE FIRST COMMANDMENT

ONE OF the scribes came up, and seeing that Jesus answered well, he asked him, Which commandment is the first of all?

Jesus replied, The first is, Hear, O Israel, the Lord our God, the Lord is one. And you shall love the Lord your God with all your heart, and with all your soul, and with all your mind, and with all your strength. The second is this, You shall love your neighbour as yourself. There is no other commandment greater than these.

And the scribe said, Well, Teacher, you have said the truth. For there is one God, and there is no other but he. And to love him with all the heart, and with all the understanding, and with all the strength, and to love one's neighbour as oneself, is more than all whole burnt offerings and sacrifices.

And when Jesus saw that he answered wisely, he said to him, You are not far from the Kingdom of God.

MARK 12:28–34

LOVE OF GOD

GOD SO loved the world, that he gave his only begotten Son, that whosoever believes in him should not perish, but have eternal life.

For God did not send the Son into the world to condemn the world, but that the world might be saved through him.

JOHN 3:16–17

THE GOOD SAMARITAN

A LAWYER stood up to test Jesus, saying, Master, what shall I do to inherit eternal life?

He said, What is written in the Law? How do you read?

He answered, You shall love the Lord your God, with all your heart, and with all your soul, and with all your strength, and with all your mind; and your neighbour as yourself.

And he said, You have answered rightly: do this, and you will live.

But he, wishing to justify himself, said to Jesus, And who is my neighbour?

Jesus answered, A man went down from Jerusalem to Jericho, and fell among thieves, who stripped him, and beat him, and went away leaving him half dead. And by chance a priest went down that way: and when he saw him, he passed by on the other side. And also a Levite, when he was at the place, came and looked at him, and passed by on the other side.

But a certain Samaritan, as he journeyed, came to where he was. And when he saw him, he had compassion on him, and went to him, and bound up his wounds, pouring on oil and wine. He put him on his own beast, and brought him to an inn, and took care of him. And the next day, he took out two silver pieces and gave them to the innkeeper, and said to him, Take care of him, and whatever you spend more, when I come again I will repay you.

Now which of these three, do you think, was neighbour to him who fell among the thieves?

He said, He that showed mercy to him.

Then Jesus said, Go, and do likewise.

LUKE 10:25–37

CHILDREN COME TO JESUS

JESUS ASKED the disciples, What were you disputing among yourselves on the way? But they held their peace, for on the way they had disputed among themselves, who was the greatest.

And he sat down, and called the twelve, and said to them, If any one would be first, he must be last of all, and servant of all. And he took a child and put him in the midst of them, and taking him in his arms he said, Whosoever shall receive one of such children in my name, receives me. And whosoever receives me, receives not me but him that sent me.

MARK 9:33–37

THEY BROUGHT young children to him, that he should touch them. But his disciples rebuked those that brought them. And when Jesus saw it, he was moved with indignation, and said to them, Suffer the little children to come unto me, and forbid them not, for of such is the Kingdom of God.

Verily I say to you, Whosoever shall not receive the Kingdom of God as a little child, he shall not enter it. And he took them in his arms, put his hands upon them, and blessed them.

MARK 10:13–16

SEE THAT you do not despise one of these little ones; for I tell you that in heaven their angels always behold the face of my Father who is in heaven.

MATTHEW 18:10

THE FAMILY OF JESUS

IS BROTHERS and his mother came, and standing outside they sent and called him. And the crowd sitting about him said, Behold your mother and brothers are outside seeking you.

And he answered, Who is my mother, or my brothers? And looking round on those who sat about him he said, Behold my mother and my brothers! For whosoever shall do the will of God, the same is my brother, and my sister, and my mother.

MARK 3:31–35

THE MESSIAH

THE CHRIST AND SELF-DENIAL

JESUS WENT out with his disciples to the towns of Caesarea Philippi, and on the way he asked them, Who do men say that I am? And they answered, John the Baptist. But some say, Elijah. And others, One of the prophets. And he said, But who do you say that I am?

And Peter answered, You are the Christ. And he charged them to tell no one about him.

And he began to teach them that the Son of Man must suffer many things, and be rejected by the elders, and the chief priests, and the scribes, and be killed, and after three days rise again. And he said this openly. But Peter took him and began to rebuke him.

But he turned and looked at his disciples, and he rebuked Peter, saying, Get behind me, Satan, for you do not mind the things of God, but those of men.

When he had called the people, with his disciples, he said, If any one would come after me, let him deny himself, and take up his cross, and follow me. For whosoever would save his life shall lose it. But whosoever shall lose his life, for my sake and the gospel's, he shall save it.

For what shall it profit a man, to gain the whole world and lose his own soul? Or what shall one give in exchange for his soul?

MARK 8:27–36

The Christ and Self-Denial ❧ 119

PETER ANSWERED, You are the Christ, the Son of the living God.

Jesus answered, Blessed are you, Simon son of Jonah, for flesh and blood have not revealed this to you, but my Father who is in heaven. And I say to you, You are Peter, and on this rock (petra) I will build my church, and the gates of Hades shall not prevail against it. I will give you the keys of the Kingdom of Heaven, and whatever you bind on earth shall be bound in heaven, and whatever you loose on earth shall be loosed in heaven.

MATTHEW 16:16–19

COUNT THE COST

WHICH OF you, intending to build a tower, does not sit down first and count the cost, whether he has enough to finish it? Otherwise, after he has laid the foundation, and is not able to finish, all that see it begin to mock him, saying, This man began to build, and was not able to finish.

Or what king, going to make war against another king, does not sit down first and take counsel, whether he is able with ten thousand to meet him that comes against him with twenty thousand?

Or else, while the other is yet a great way off, he sends an embassy and asks for conditions of peace.
So likewise, whoever of you does not renounce all that he has, he cannot be my disciple.

LUKE 14:28–33

SIGNS FROM HEAVEN?

SOME, TO test him, sought a sign from heaven.

And when the people were gathered thick together, he began to say, This is an evil generation seeking a sign, and no sign shall be given to it, but the sign of the prophet Jonah. For as Jonah was a sign to the men of Nineveh, so shall the Son of Man be to this generation.

The queen of the south shall rise up in the judgement with the men of this generation, and condemn them: for she came from the ends of the earth to hear the wisdom of Solomon, and behold a greater than Solomon is here.

The men of Nineveh shall rise up in the judgement with this generation, and shall condemn it; for they repented at the preaching of Jonah, and behold a greater than Jonah is here.

LUKE 11:16,29–32

HE SAID also to the people, When you see a cloud rising in the west, straightaway you say, A shower is coming, and so it is.

And when you see a south wind blow, you say, There will be a scorching heat, and so it happens.

You hypocrites, you know how to interpret the face of the sky and the earth, but why is it that you do not know how to interpret this time?

LUKE 12:54–57

EVIL POWERS

HE WAS casting out a demon of dumbness, and it came to pass that when the demon had gone the man spoke. The people marvelled, but some of them said, He casts out demons by Beelzebub, the prince of demons. But knowing their thoughts, he said to them, Every kingdom divided against itself becomes desolate, and a house divided against itself falls. So if Satan is divided against himself, how shall his kingdom stand? For you say that I cast out demons by Beelzebub. But if I cast out demons by Beelzebub, by whom do your sons cast them out? Therefore they shall be your judges. But if I cast out demons by the finger of God, then the Kingdom of God has come upon you indeed.

When a strong man, well armed, guards his own palace, his goods are in peace. But if a stronger than he comes upon him and overcomes him, he takes away all the armour in which he trusted and divides the plunder.

When an unclean spirit has gone out of a man, he passes through dry places seeking rest. Finding none, he says, I will return to my house from which I came. And when he comes he finds it swept and garnished. Then he goes and brings seven other spirits more wicked than himself, and they enter and dwell there. And the last state of that man is worse than the first.

As he said these things, a woman in the crowd raised her voice and said, Blessed is the womb that bore you and the breasts that you sucked. But he said, Blessed rather are those who hear the word of God and keep it.

LUKE 11:14–28

JOHN (THE DISCIPLE) said, Master, we saw a man casting out demons in your name, and we forbade him because he did not follow us. But Jesus said, Do not forbid him, for no one can do a mighty work in my name and can lightly speak evil of me. For he that is not against us is for us.

Whosoever shall give you a cup of water to drink, because you belong to Christ, verily I tell you he shall not lose his reward.

MARK 9:38–41

THE RICH MAN AND THE KINGDOM OF GOD

A MAN came running, and kneeled to him, and asked him, Good Master, what shall I do to inherit eternal life? Jesus said, Why do you call me good? There is none good but one, that is, God. You know the commandments, Do not kill, Do not commit adultery, Do not steal, Do not bear false witness, Do not defraud, Honour your father and mother.

And he answered, Master, I have observed all these things from my youth.

Then Jesus, looking at him, loved him, and said, One thing you lack: go your way, sell whatever you have, and give it to the poor, and you will have treasure in heaven: and come and follow me.

But he was sad at that saying, and he went away sorrowful, for he had great possessions.

And Jesus looked round about, and said to his disciples, How hard it is for those that have riches to enter the Kingdom of God. And the disciples were astonished at his words.

But Jesus said again, Children, how hard it is for those who trust in riches to enter the Kingdom of God. It is easier for a camel to go through the eye of a needle, than for a rich man to enter the Kingdom of God. And they were astonished beyond measure, saying, Then who can be saved? And Jesus looking at them said, With men it is impossible, but not with God, for with God all things are possible.

Then Peter began to say, Lo, we have left all, and have followed you.

And Jesus answered, Verily, I tell you, There is no one who has left house, or brothers, or sisters, or mother, or father, or children, or lands, for my sake and the gospel's, But he shall receive a hundredfold now in this time, houses, and brothers, and sisters, and mothers, and children, and lands, with persecutions, and in the world to come eternal life. But many that are first shall be last, and the last first.

MARK 10:17–31

BE READY

LET YOUR loins be girded, and your lamps burning, and be like men waiting for their Lord returning from a wedding, that when he comes and knocks, they may open up immediately.

Blessed are those servants whom the lord finds watching when he comes: verily, I tell you, he will gird himself, and make them sit down at table, and will come and serve them. And if he comes in the second watch, or the third, and finds them so, blessed are those servants.

Know this, that if the master of the house had known at what time the thief was coming, he would have watched, and would not have left his house to be broken into.

Therefore, be ready, for the Son of Man is coming at a time that you do not expect.

LUKE 12:35–40

TREASURE ON EARTH

ONE OF the company said to him, Master, speak to my brother, that he may divide the inheritance with me.

But he said, Man, who made me a judge or a divider over you? And he said to them, Take heed, and beware of covetousness, for a man's life does not consist in the abundance of the things which he possesses.

He spoke a parable to them, saying, The land of a rich man brought forth plentifully, and he thought to himself, What shall I do, because I have nowhere to put all my fruits?

And he said, I will do this: I will pull down my barns and build greater ones; and there I will store all my corn and my goods.

And I will say to my soul, Soul, you have many goods laid up for many years; take your ease, eat, drink, and be merry.

But God said to him, You foolish one, your soul will be required of you this night: and the things which you have prepared, whose shall they be?

So is he that lays up treasure for himself, and is not rich towards God.

LUKE 12:13–21

PARABLES OF ACTION

UNJUST STEWARD

THERE WAS a rich man who had a steward who was accused of wasting his goods. So he called him and said, What is this that I hear of you? Give an account of your stewardship, for you can no longer be steward.

Then the steward said to himself, What shall I do, for my lord is taking the stewardship away from me? I cannot dig. I am ashamed to beg. I have resolved what to do, so that when I am put out of the stewardship they may receive me into their homes.

So he called each one of his lord's debtors, and said to the first, How much do you owe my lord? He said, A hundred measures of oil. Then he said to him, Take your bill, and sit down quickly, and write fifty. Then he said to another, And how much do you owe? He said, A hundred measures of wheat. And he said, Take your bill and write eighty.

And the lord commended the unjust steward, because he had done wisely. For the children of this world are wiser in their own generation than the children of light.

And I tell you, Make friends by the unrighteous Mammon, so that when it fails they may receive you into the eternal habitations.

He that is faithful in what is least, is faithful also in much; and he that is unjust in the least is also unjust in much.

If you have not been faithful in the unrighteous Mammon, who will commit the true riches to your trust? And if you have not been faithful in that which is another's, who will give you that which is your own?

LUKE 16:1–12

RICH MAN AND LAZARUS

THERE WAS a rich man, who was clothed in purple and fine linen, and fared sumptuously every day. And a beggar named Lazarus, full of sores, was laid at his gate. He desired to be fed with the crumbs which fell from the rich man's table, and even the dogs came and licked his sores. And it came to pass that the beggar died, and was carried by the angels to Abraham's bosom.

The rich man also died and was buried. And in Hades, being in torments, he saw Abraham far off and Lazarus in his bosom. And he cried out, Father Abraham, have mercy on me. Send Lazarus to dip the tip of his finger in water to cool my tongue, for I am tormented in this flame.

But Abraham said, Son, remember that in your lifetime you received good things, and Lazarus evil things. But now he is comforted, and you are tormented. And besides this, between us and you there is a great gulf fixed: so that those who would pass from here to you cannot do it, neither can they cross over from thence to us.

And he said, Then I pray you, father, that you would send him to my father's house, for I have five brothers, so that he may warn them, lest they also come to this place of torment. Abraham said, They have Moses and the prophets, let them hear them.

And he said, No, father Abraham, but if one goes to them from the dead they will repent.

And he said, If they do not hear Moses and the prophets, neither will they be persuaded if someone rose from the dead.

LUKE 16:19–31

WOE TO THE RICH

WOE TO you that are rich, for you have received your
consolation.
Woe to you that are full now, for you will hunger.
Woe to you that laugh now, for you will mourn and weep.
Woe to you when everyone speaks well of you, for so did their
fathers to the false prophets.

LUKE 6:24–26

DINNER GUESTS

JESUS TOLD a parable to those who were invited, when he noticed how they chose the best places, saying to them,

When you are invited to a wedding, do not sit down in the highest place, unless a more honourable man than you is invited. And he who invited both you and him will come and say to you, Give the place to this man, and you begin with shame to take the lowest place.

But when you are bidden, go and sit down in the lowest place, so that when he that invited you comes, he may say to you, Friend, go up higher. Then you will be honoured by all those who sit at table with you.

For whosoever exalts himself shall be humbled: and he that humbles himself shall be exalted.

Then he said to the one who had invited him, When you give a dinner or a supper, do not invite your friends, nor your brothers, nor your kinsmen, nor rich neighbours, lest they invite you back and reward you. But when you give a feast, call the poor, the maimed, the lame, the blind. And you will be blessed, for they cannot repay you. You will be repaid at the resurrection of the just.

LUKE 14:7–14

THE GREAT SUPPER

WHEN ONE of those who sat at table with Jesus heard him, he said, Blessed is he that shall eat bread in the Kingdom of God.

Then Jesus said to him, There was a man who made a great supper and invited many. And at supper time he sent his servant to tell those who were invited, Come, for everything is now ready. And they all with one accord began to make excuses.

The first said, I have bought a field, and I must go and see it, I pray you, have me excused. And another said, I have bought five yoke of oxen, and I must go to check them. I pray you, have me excused. And another said, I have married a wife, and therefore I cannot come. So the servant came and told his lord these things.

Then the master of the house was angry and said to his servant, Go out quickly into the streets and lanes of the city, and bring in here the poor, and the maimed, and the lame, and the blind.

And the servant said, Lord, it is done as you commanded, and still there is room. And the lord said, Go out into the highways and hedges, and compel them to come in, that my house may be filled.

For I tell you, that none of those who were bidden shall taste my supper.

LUKE 14:15–24

HOW OFTEN TO FORGIVE

ETER CAME up and said, Lord, how often shall my brother sin against me, and I forgive him? Until seven times?

Jesus said, I do not say, Until seven times; but, until seventy times seven. Therefore the Kingdom of Heaven may be likened to a king who wished to settle accounts with his servants. And when he began to reckon, one man was brought to him who owed ten thousand gold pieces. But as he could not pay, his lord commanded him to be sold, and his wife and children, and all that he had, and payment to be made. Then the servant fell down, beseeching him and saying, Lord have patience with me, and I will pay you everything. Then the lord was moved with compassion, and released the servant and forgave him the debt.

But the same servant went out, and found one of his fellow-servants who owed him a hundred pence, and he caught hold of him, and took him by the throat, saying, Pay me what you owe. And the fellow-servant fell down at his feet, and pleaded with him, Have patience with me, and I will pay you everything. And he would not, but went and threw him into prison, till he should pay the debt. So when his fellow-servants saw what had happened, they were very sorry, and went and told their lord all that was done.

Then his lord, when he had called him, said to him, You wicked servant, I forgave you all that debt, because you pleaded with me. Should you not also have had compassion on your fellow-servant, as I had pity on you? And his lord was angry, and delivered him to the tormentors, until he should pay all that was due. So my heavenly Father will do to you, if you do not forgive your brother from your heart.

MATTHEW 18:21–35

TWO OR THREE TOGETHER

IF YOUR brother sins against you, go and tell him his fault between you and him alone. If he listens to you, you have gained your brother. But if he will not listen, take one or two others with you, that every word may be established by two or three witnesses. If he refuses to hear them, tell it to the church. And if he refuses to hear the church, let him be to you like a Gentile or a publican.

Verily I say to you, whatever you bind on earth shall be bound in heaven, and whatever you loose on earth shall be loosed in heaven.

Again I say to you, If two of you agree on earth about anything that they shall ask, it shall be done for them by my Father in heaven. For where two or three are gathered in my name, I am there in the midst of them.

MATTHEW 18:15–20

JESUS SAID, Where there are two, they are not without God. And where there is one alone, I say, I am with him.

Raise the stone, and you will find me;
Split the wood, and I am there.

PAPYRUS FRAGMENTS OF SAYINGS OF JESUS, FROM OXYRHYNCHUS IN
EGYPT

STATUS OR SERVICE

JAMES AND John (disciples) came to Jesus saying, Master, we want you to do for us whatever we shall ask. And he said, What do you want me to do for you? They replied, Grant that we may sit, one at your right hand, and one at your left, in your glory.

But Jesus said, You do not know what you are asking. Can you drink of the cup that I drink of, or be baptized with the baptism that I am baptized with?

And they said, We can.

Jesus replied, You shall indeed drink of the cup that I drink of, and be baptized with the baptism with which I am baptized. But to sit at my right hand or my left hand is not mine to give, but it is for those for whom it has been prepared.

And when the ten (disciples) heard this they began to be indignant with James and John. But Jesus called them to him and said, You know that those who rule over the Gentiles lord it over them; and their great ones exercise authority over them. But it shall not be so among you: for whosoever would be great among you must be your servant, and whosoever would be first among you must be servant of all.

For even the Son of Man came not to be served, but to serve, and to give his life as a ransom for many.

MARK 10:35–45

THE LABOURERS IN THE VINEYARD

THE KINGDOM of Heaven is like a householder who went out early in the morning to hire labourers for his vineyard. And when he had agreed with the labourers for a day's wage, he sent them into his vineyard.

And he went out about the third hour, and saw others standing idle in the market place. And he said to them: Go also into the vineyard and whatsoever is right I will give you. And they went there. He went out about the sixth and ninth hour and did likewise. And he went out about the eleventh hour and found some others standing idle, and he asked them, Why are you standing here idle all the day? They replied, Because no one has hired us. He said to them, You go also into the vineyard, and you will receive whatever is right.

So when the evening came, the master of the vineyard said to his steward, Call the labourers and give them their hire, beginning from the last unto the first. When those hired about the eleventh hour came, each of them received a day's wage. But when the first came, they supposed that they should have received more, and each also received a day's wage. When they had received it, they murmured against the master of the house, saying, These last have worked only one hour, and you have made them equal to us who have borne the burden and heat of the day.

But he answered one of them, Friend, I am doing you no wrong. Did you not agree with me for a day's wage? Take what is yours, and go. I will give unto this last, even as unto you. Is it not lawful for me to do what I want with my own? Is your eye evil, because I am good?

So the last shall be first, and the first last.

MATTHEW 20:1–16

PARABLE OF THE GOLD PIECES

I<small>T WILL</small> be as when a man travelling to a far country, called his servants and delivered to them his goods. To one he gave five gold pieces, to another two, and to another one; to each according to his ability, and then he went away.

Then he that had received five gold pieces went and traded with them and made five gold pieces more. And he that had received two gained two gold pieces more. But he that had received one, went and dug in the ground and hid his master's money.

After a long time the Master of those servants came back, and reckoned with them. So he that had received five gold pieces came and brought five gold pieces more, saying, Master, you gave me five gold pieces, see, I have gained five gold pieces more. His master said, Well done, good and faithful servant. You have been faithful over a few things, I will make you ruler over many; enter into the joy of your lord.

He that had received two gold pieces also came and said, Master, you gave me two gold pieces, see I have gained two gold pieces more. His master said, Well done, good and faithful servant. You have been faithful over a few things, I will make you ruler over many; enter into the joy of your lord.

Then he who had received one gold piece came and said,

Master, I knew that you are a hard man, reaping where you have not sown, and gathering where you did not scatter. So I was afraid, and went and hid your gold piece in the ground. There, you have your own.

His master answered, You wicked and lazy servant. You knew that I reap where I have not sown, and gather where I have not scattered? Then you ought to have put my money with the bankers, and at my coming I should have received my own with interest. So take the gold piece from him and give it to him who has ten gold pieces. For, to everyone that has, more will be given and he will have abundance. But from him who has not, even what he has shall be taken away. And cast the unprofitable servant into outer darkness, where there shall be weeping and gnashing of teeth.

MATTHEW 25:14–30/LUKE 19:12–27

GOING TO JERUSALEM

A SAVED TAX COLLECTOR

J ESUS ENTERED and was passing through Jericho. And there was a man named Zacchaeus, a chief tax collector, and he was rich. And he wanted to see who Jesus was, and could not in the crowd because he was small in height. And he ran on in front and climbed up into a sycamore tree to see him as he passed that way.

And when Jesus came to the place he looked up and said to him, Zacchaeus, make haste and come down, for today I must stay at your house. And he made haste, and came down, and received him joyfully. And when people saw it they murmured, saying, He has gone to be the guest of a man that is a sinner.

And Zacchaeus stood and said to the Lord, Behold Lord, I am giving half my goods to the poor, and if I have taken anything from anyone, I shall restore it fourfold.

And Jesus said to him, Today salvation has come to this house, since he also is a son of Abraham. For the Son of Man came to seek and save that which was lost.

LUKE 19:1–10

O JERUSALEM

THERE WERE some present who told him of Galileans whose blood Pilate had mingled with their sacrifices.

Jesus answered, Do you suppose that these Galileans were worse sinners than all the other Galileans, because they suffered such things? I tell you, No. But unless you repent you will all perish likewise.

Or those eighteen upon whom the tower in Siloam fell and killed them; do you think that they were worse offenders than all the others who lived in Jerusalem? I tell you, No. But unless you repent you will all perish likewise.

LUKE 13:1–5

A T THAT same time some Pharisees came and said to him, Go away from here, for Herod wants to kill you. And he said, Go and tell that fox, I cast out demons and perform cures today, and tomorrow, and on the third day I shall finish. But I must go on my way today, and tomorrow, and the next day, for it cannot be that a prophet should perish away from Jerusalem.

O Jerusalem, Jerusalem, killing the prophets and stoning those that are sent to you! How often would I have gathered your children together, as a hen gathers her brood under her wings, but you would not. Behold your house is left desolate. Verily, I say to you, you will not see me, until you say, Blessed is he that comes in the name of the Lord.

LUKE 13:31–35

ENTRY INTO JERUSALEM

WHEN THEY came near to Jerusalem, he sent two of his disciples and said to them, Go into the village opposite you and as you enter it you will find a young donkey tied, on which no one has ever sat; loose it and bring it. And if anyone says to you, Why are you doing this? say, The Lord needs it, and at once he will send it here.

They went away and found it as he had told them. And they brought the donkey to Jesus and put their garments on it and he sat on it. And many spread their garments in the way, and others cut down branches off the trees and strewed them on the road. And those who went in front, and those that followed cried, Hosanna! Blessed is he who comes in the name of the Lord. Blessed be the kingdom of our father David that is coming. Hosanna in the highest!

MARK 11:1–10

ALL THIS was done that it might be fulfilled which was spoken by the prophet, saying, Behold, thy King comes to thee, meek, and sitting upon an ass.

MATTHEW 21:4–5

SOME OF the Pharisees in the crowd said to him, Master, rebuke your disciples.

He answered, I tell you that if these should hold their peace, the very stones would cry out. And when he came near he saw the city, and he wept over it, saying, If you had known, even today, the things which make for peace! But now they are hidden from your eyes. For the days shall come upon you when your enemies shall cast up a bank about you, and compass you round, and keep you in on every side. And they will dash you to the ground, and your children with you, and they will not leave one stone upon another, because you did not know the time of your visitation.

LUKE 19:39–44

CLEANSING THE TEMPLE

THEY CAME to Jerusalem and Jesus went into the temple, and began to drive out those who sold and those who bought in the temple, and overturned the tables of the money-changers, and the seats of those who sold doves, and he would not allow anyone to carry anything through the temple. And he taught, saying to them, Is it not written, My house shall be called a house of prayer, for all nations? But you have made it a den of thieves.

And as he was walking in the temple, there came to him the chief priests and scribes and elders, and they asked him, By what authority are you doing these things, or who gave you this authority to do them? And Jesus said to them, I will ask you a question, and if you answer I will tell you by what authority I do these things. The baptism of John, was it from heaven, or from men? Answer me. But they argued among themselves, If we say, From heaven, he will say, Then why did you not believe him? But if we say, From men, they feared the people; for all held that John was a true prophet. So they answered Jesus, We cannot tell. And Jesus replied, Neither will I tell you by what authority I do these things.

MARK 11:15–17, 27–33

THE PRIESTS AND ELDERS PLOT

THEN THE chief priests and the Pharisees gathered a council and said, What shall we do? For this man does many signs. If we leave him alone, everyone will believe in him. And the Romans will come and destroy our place and our nation.

And one of them, Caiaphas, who was high priest that year, said to them, You know nothing at all, nor do you consider that it is expedient for you that one man should die for the people, and that the whole nation should not perish. And this he did not say of himself, but being high priest that year, he prophesied that Jesus should die for the nation; and not for that nation only, but also that he should gather together into one the children of God who were scattered abroad. So from that day they took counsel how to put him to death.

JOHN 11:47–53

FIG TREE

Jesus spoke also this parable: A man had a fig tree planted in his vineyard, but when he came seeking fruit from it he found none. Then he said to the vinedresser, See, for three years I have sought fruit from this fig tree and have found none. Cut it down, why should it waste the ground? But he answered, Master, leave it this year too, till I dig about it and put on manure. Then if it bears fruit, well and good; but if not, you can cut it down.

LUKE 13:6–9

VINEYARD AND TENANTS

A MAN planted a vineyard, and set a hedge about it, and dug a pit for the winepress, and built a tower, and let it out to tenants and went into a far country. And when the season came he sent a servant to the tenants, that he might receive the fruit of the vineyard. And they caught him, and beat him, and sent him away empty. Again he sent another servant, and they wounded him in the head and handled him shamefully. Then he sent another, and him they killed, and many others; beating some, and killing some. He had yet one, a beloved son, and he sent him last to them, saying, They will reverence my son.

But those tenants said among themselves, This is the heir; come, let us kill him, and the inheritance will be ours. And they took him, and killed him, and cast him out of the vineyard.

What then will the owner of the vineyard do? He will come and destroy the tenants, and give the vineyard to others.

Have you not read this scripture: The stone which the builders rejected, has become the head of the corner? This was the Lord's doing, and it is marvellous in our eyes.

MARK 12:1–11

RESURRECTION

THERE CAME to Jesus some Sadducees, those who say that there is no resurrection, and they asked him, saying, Master, Moses wrote for us that if a man's brother dies, having a wife but no children, his brother should take his wife to have children for his brother. Now there were seven brothers, and the first took a wife, and died without children. The second and the third took her, and in the same way all seven left no children and died. Last of all the woman died. Therefore, in the resurrection, whose wife will she be? For the seven had her as wife.

Jesus answered, The children of this world marry, and are given in marriage. But those who are counted worthy to attain to that world, and to the resurrection from the dead, neither marry nor are given in marriage. Neither can they die any more, for they are equal to the angels. They are children of God, being children of the resurrection.

But that the dead are raised, even Moses showed this in the passage about the Bush, where he called the Lord the God of Abraham, and the God of Isaac, and the God of Jacob. He is not a God of the dead, but of the living; for all are alive to him.

LUKE 20:27–38

JESUS SAID to Martha, Your brother will rise again. Martha replied, I know that he will rise again in the resurrection at the last day.

Jesus said, I am the resurrection and the life; he who believes in me, though he die, yet shall he live. And whosoever lives and believes in me shall never die.

JOHN 11:23–26

CAESAR AND GOD

THEY SENT some of the Pharisees and Herodians, to catch him in his talk. And they came and said, Teacher, we know that you are true, and care for no one: for you do not regard the person of men, but teach the way of God in truth: Is it lawful to pay taxes to Caesar, or not? Shall we pay them, or shall we not?

But knowing their hypocrisy, he said to them: Why do you tempt me? Bring me a coin, that I may see it. And they brought one. And he asked them, Whose is this likeness and inscription? They replied, Caesar's. And Jesus answered, Render to Caesar the things that are Caesar's, and to God the things that are God's.

MARK 12:13–17

WHILE JESUS taught in the temple he asked, How can the scribes say that Christ is the Son of David? For David himself said, by the Holy Spirit, The Lord said to my Lord, sit at my right hand, till I put thy enemies under thy feet.

David himself calls him Lord. So how can he be his son?

MARK 12:35–37

JESUS SAT down opposite the treasury, and he saw how people put money into the treasury. And many of the rich put in much. And a poor widow came, and put in two copper coins. And he called his disciples and said to them, Verily I tell you, this poor widow has put in more than all those who are giving to the treasury. For they all put in from their abundance, but she of her want has put in all that she had, even all her living.

MARK 12:41–44

BLINDNESS AND THE LIGHT OF THE WORLD

A S JESUS passed by, he saw a man blind from birth. And his disciples asked him, Rabbi, who sinned, this man or his parents, that he was born blind?

Jesus answered, Neither did this man sin, nor his parents: but that the works of God might be shown in him. We must do the works of him that sent me, while it is day. The night is coming, when no one can work. As long as I am in the world, I am the light of the world.

When he had said this, he spat on the ground, and made clay with the spittle, and he anointed the man's eyes with the clay, and said to him, Go and wash in the pool of Siloam. He went away and washed, and came back seeing.

His neighbours, and those who had seen him before as a beggar, said, Is not this he that sat and begged? Some said, It is he: others said, No, but he is like him. He said, I am he. They said, Then how were your eyes opened? He answered, The man called Jesus made clay, and anointed my eyes, and said, Go to Siloam and wash. So I went and washed, and received sight. They said, Where is he? He said, I do not know.

They said to the blind man again, What do you say about him, since he opened your eyes? He said, He is a prophet.

They called the man who had been blind a second time and said to him, Give the praise to God, we know that this man is a sinner. He answered, Whether he is a sinner or not, I do not know. One thing I know, that whereas I was blind, now I see.

They said to him, You were altogether born in sin, and would you teach us? And they cast him out.

Jesus heard that they had cast him out, and finding him he said, Do you believe in the Son of Man? He said, Who is he, sir, that I may believe in him? Jesus said, You have both seen him and it is he who is speaking to you. He said, Lord, I believe, and he worshipped him.

JOHN 9:1–12,17,24–25,34–38

THE HOUR HAS COME

THERE WERE some Greeks among those who went to worship at the festival. These came to Philip, who was from Bethsaida in Galilee, and said to him, Sir, we want to see Jesus. Philip went and told Andrew, and Andrew and Philip told Jesus.

Jesus said, The hour has come, for the Son of Man to be glorified. Verily, verily, I say to you, Unless a grain of wheat falls into the ground and dies, it remains alone; but if it dies, it bears much fruit. He that loves his life loses it, and he that hates his life in this world will keep it for eternal life.

If any one serves me, let him follow me, and where I am, there my servant will be also. If any one serves me, my Father will honour him.

Now is the judgement of this world, now the prince of this world will be cast out. And I, when I am lifted up from the earth, will draw everyone to myself.

Jesus cried and said, He who believes in me, believes not in me but in him that sent me. And he that sees me sees him that sent me. I have come as light into the world, that whoever believes in me should not remain in darkness.

And if any one hears my words, and does not believe them, I do not judge him. For I did not come to judge the world, but to save the world.

He who rejects me, and does not receive my words, has one that judges him: the word that I have spoken will judge him on the last day. For I have not spoken from myself; but the Father who sent me gave me commandment, what to say and what to speak. And I know that his commandment is eternal life. Therefore whatever I speak, I speak as the Father has told me.

JOHN 12:20–26,31–32,44–50

COMING TRIALS
AND JUDGEMENT

ON THAT DAY

H E SAID to the disciples, The days will come when you will desire to see one of the days of the Son of Man, and shall not see it. They will say to you, See here! or See there! But do not go after them or follow them.

For as the lightning flashes from one part under heaven and shines to the other part, so shall the Son of Man be in his day. But first he must suffer many things, and be rejected by this generation. As it was in the days of Noah, so shall it be in the days of the Son of Man. They ate, they drank, they married, they were given in marriage, until the day that Noah entered the ark, and the flood came and destroyed them all.

Likewise, as it was in the days of Lot. They ate, they drank, they bought, they sold, they planted, they built. But on the day that Lot went out of Sodom, it rained fire and brimstone from heaven and destroyed them all.

So will it be on the day that the Son of Man is revealed. On that day, if one is on the housetop and his goods in the house, let him not come down to take them away. Likewise he that is in the field, let him not return home. Remember Lot's wife. Whosoever shall seek to save his life shall lose it; and whosoever shall lose his life shall preserve it,

I tell you, in that night there will be two men in one bed; one shall be taken, and the other left.

Two women will be grinding corn together; one shall be taken and the other left.

They said to him, Where, Lord? He answered, Wherever the body is, there the vultures will be gathered together.

LUKE 17:22–37

SIGNS OF THE TIMES

AS JESUS went out of the temple, one of his disciples said to him, Master, see what fine stones and what fine buildings! And Jesus answered, You see these great buildings? There shall not be left one stone upon another, that shall not be thrown down.

And as he sat on the Mount of Olives opposite the temple, Peter and James and John and Andrew asked him privately, Tell us, when will this be? And what shall be the sign when these things are all to be fulfilled?

And Jesus answered, Take heed that no one leads you astray. For many shall come in my name, saying, I am he, and they will lead many astray. But when you hear of wars and rumours of wars, do not be troubled. Such things must happen, but the end is not yet. For nation shall rise against nation, and kingdom against kingdom: there shall be earthquakes in various places, and there shall be famines: these are the beginnings of sorrows.

Take heed to yourselves. When they lead you to trial, do not be anxious beforehand what you are to speak, but speak whatever is given to you in that hour, for it is not you that speak but the Holy Spirit.

In those days, after that tribulation, the sun shall be darkened, and the moon shall not give its light. The stars shall fall from heaven, and the powers in heaven shall be shaken. And then they shall see the Son of Man coming in clouds, with great power and glory. And then he will send out the angels, and gather his elect from the four winds, from the ends of the earth to the end of heaven.

Now learn a parable from the fig tree. When its branch is tender, and puts forth leaves, you know that summer is near. In the same way, when you see these things happen, know that he is near, even at the door. Verily, I tell you, this generation will not pass away, before all these things take place. Heaven and earth shall pass away: but my words shall not pass away.

MARK 13:1–8,11,24–31

WISE AND FOOLISH MAIDENS

THE KINGDOM of Heaven shall be likened to ten maidens, who took their lamps and went to meet the bridegroom. Five of them were foolish, and five were wise. Those that were foolish took their lamps, but took no oil with them. But the wise took oil in vessels with their lamps.

Now while the bridegroom tarried, they all slumbered and slept. And at midnight there was a cry made, Behold, the bridegroom! Come out to meet him.

Then all those maidens arose and trimmed their lamps. And the foolish said to the wise, Give us some of your oil, for our lamps are going out. But the wise answered, Perhaps there will not be enough for us and you. Go rather to those who sell and buy for yourselves.

And while they went to buy, the bridegroom came, and those who were ready went in with him to the marriage feast. And the door was shut. Afterwards the other maidens came also, saying, Lord, Lord, open to us. But he answered, Verily I tell you, I do not know you.

Watch therefore, for you do not know either the day or the hour.

MATTHEW 25:1–13

THEREFORE BE also ready, for the Son of Man is coming at an hour that you do not think.

Who then is a faithful and wise servant, whom his lord has made ruler over his household, to give them food in due season? Blessed is that servant whom his lord when he comes will find so doing. Verily, I tell you, he will set him over all that he has.

MATTHEW 24:44–47

JUDGEMENT BY DEEDS

WHEN THE Son of Man comes in his glory, and all the angels with him, then he will sit on the throne of his glory. All nations will be gathered before him, and he will separate them one from another, as a shepherd separates the sheep from the goats.

Then the King will say to those at his right hand, Come, you blessed of my Father, inherit the kingdom prepared for you from the foundation of the world. For I was hungry, and you gave me food; I was thirsty, and you gave me drink; I was a stranger, and you took me in; naked, and you clothed me; I was sick, and you visited me; I was in prison, and you came to me.

Then the righteous will answer him, saying, Lord, when did we see you hungry, and fed you? Or thirsty, and gave you drink? When did we see you a stranger, and took you in? Or naked, and clothed you? When did we see you sick, or in prison, and came to you?

And the King will answer, Verily, I tell you, inasmuch as you did it to one of the least of these my brothers, you did it to me.

Then he will say to those at his left hand, Depart from me, you cursed, into eternal fire, prepared for the devil and his angels. For I was hungry, and you gave me no food; I was thirsty and you gave me no drink; I was a stranger, and you did not take me in; naked, and you did not clothe me; sick and in prison, and you did not visit me.

Then they also will answer, saying, Lord, when did we see you hungry, or thirsty, or a stranger, or naked, or sick, or in prison, and did not minister to you?

Then he will answer, Verily, I tell you, inasmuch as you did not do it to one of the least of these, you did not do it to me.

And these will go away into eternal punishment, but the righteous to eternal life.

MATTHEW 25:31–46

THE LAST SUPPER

FOOT-WASHING

WHEN EVENING came, he sat at table with the twelve disciples.

Jesus rose from supper, laid aside his garments, and took a towel to gird himself. Then he poured water into a basin, and began to wash the disciples' feet and to wipe them with the towel.

He came to Simon Peter, and Peter said to him, Lord, do you wash my feet? Jesus answered, What I am doing you do not know now, but you will understand afterwards. Peter said, You shall never wash my feet. Jesus answered, If I do not wash you, you have no part in me. Peter said, Lord, not my feet only, but also my hands and my head.

Jesus said, He that is bathed needs only to wash his feet and is clean. And you are clean, but not all of you. For he knew who would betray him, and so he said, You are not all clean.

So after he had washed their feet, and had taken his garments and sat down, he said to them, Do you know what I have done to you? You call me Master and Lord, and you say well, for so I am. If I then, your Lord and Master, have washed your feet, you also ought to wash one another's feet. For I have given you an example, that you should do as I have done to you. Verily, verily, I say to you, A servant is not greater than his master, neither is one that is sent greater than he that sent him. If you know these things, blessed are you if you do them.

A new commandment I give you, that you love one another. Even as I have loved you, that you also love one another. By this everybody will know that you are my disciples, if you have love for one another.

MATTHEW 26:20; JOHN 13:4–17, 34–35

UNTROUBLED HEARTS

LET NOT your hearts be troubled: believe in God, believe also in me. In my Father's house are many mansions. If it were not so, would I have told you that I go to prepare a place for you? And when I go and prepare a place for you, I will come again and receive you to myself; that where I am, you may be also. And you know the way where I am going.

Thomas said to him, Lord, we do not know where you are going; how can we know the way?

Jesus said to him, I am the way, and the truth, and the life. No one comes to the Father, but by me. If you had known me, you would have known my Father also: from henceforth you know him and have seen him.

Philip said to him, Lord, show us the Father, and it will be enough.

Jesus said to him, Have I been with you so long, Philip, and you do not know me? He that has seen me has seen the Father. How can you say, Show us the Father?

Do you not believe that I am in the Father, and the Father in me? The words that I say to you I do not speak from myself, but the Father who abides in me does his deeds. Believe me that I am in the Father, and the Father in me; or else believe me from the deeds themselves.

Verily, verily, I say to you, he who believes in me will do the deeds that I do; and he will do greater deeds than these because I am going to the Father.

Whatsoever you shall ask in my name, I will do it, that the Father may be glorified in the Son. If you ask anything in my name, I will do it.

Peace I leave with you, my peace I give you. Not as the world gives do I give it to you. Let not your hearts be troubled, neither let them be afraid.

JOHN 14:1–14,27

THE HOLY SPIRIT

IF YOU love me, you will keep my commandments. And I will pray the Father, and he will give you another Counsellor, that he may be with you for ever, even the Spirit of truth, whom the world cannot receive, because it neither sees him nor knows him. But you know him, for he dwells with you, and will be in you.

The Counsellor, the Holy Spirit, whom the Father will send in my name, will teach you all things, and he will bring to your remembrance all that I have said to you.

It is expedient for you that I go away, for if I do not go away the Counsellor will not come to you; but if I go, I will send him to you. And when he comes he will convince the world of sin, and righteousness, and judgement. Of sin, because they do not believe in me. Of righteousness, because I am going to the Father and you will see me no more. Of judgement, because the ruler of this world is judged.

I have many things to say to you still, but you cannot bear them now. But when he, the Spirit of truth, has come, he will guide you into all the truth, for he will not speak from himself, but whatever he hears he shall speak, and he will show you things to come. He will glorify me, for he will take what is mine and show it to you.

These things I have spoken to you, that in me you may have peace. In the world you have tribulation; but be of good cheer, I have overcome the world.

JOHN 14:15–17, 26; 16:7–14, 33

THE TRUE VINE

I AM the true vine, and my Father is the vinedresser. Every branch of mine that bears no fruit, he takes away. And every branch that bears fruit, he prunes it, that it may bear more fruit. You are clean already by the word which I have spoken to you.

Abide in me, and I in you. As the branch cannot bear fruit by itself, unless it abides in the vine, neither can you unless you abide in me. I am the vine, you are the branches. He that abides in me, and I in him, he bears much fruit, for without me you can do nothing. If he does not abide in me, he is cast forth as a branch and is withered, and the branches are gathered together, cast into the fire and burnt. If you abide in me, and my words abide in you, ask whatever you will and it shall be done for you.

This is my commandment, that you love one another, as I have loved you. Greater love has no one than this, that he lay down his life for his friends. You are my friends, if you do whatever I command you. Henceforth I do not call you servants, for the servant does not know what his master is doing. But I have called you friends, for all that I have heard from my Father I have made known to you. You did not choose me, but I chose you, and appointed you that you should go and bear fruit and that your fruit should remain: so that whatever you ask the Father in my name, he may give it to you. This I command you, that you love one another.

JOHN 15:1–17

ETERNAL LIFE

JESUS SPOKE these words, and lifting up his eyes to heaven he said, Father, the hour has come; glorify thy Son, that the Son may glorify thee, as thou hast given him power over all flesh, that he may give eternal life to all whom thou hast given him.

This is eternal life, that they should know thee, the only true God, and Jesus Christ whom thou hast sent.

I glorified thee on earth, I have finished the work which thou gavest me to do. And now, Father, glorify me with thine own self, with the glory which I had with thee before the world was made.

I have manifested thy name to the men whom thou gavest me out of the world. They were thine, and thou gavest them to me, and they have kept thy word.

I do not pray that thou shouldst take them out of the world, but that thou shouldst keep them from evil. Sanctify them in the truth: thy word is truth.

I do not pray for these alone, but also for those who will believe in me through their word: that they may all be one, as thou Father art in me and I in thee, that they also may be in us; so that the world may believe that thou hast sent me.

And the glory which thou hast given to me I have given to them; that they may be one, even as we are one. I in them, and thou in me, that they may be perfectly in one. That the world may know that thou hast sent me, and hast loved them even as thou hast loved me.

JOHN 17·1–6,15,20–23

THE LORD'S SUPPER

A S THEY were eating Jesus took bread, and blessed and broke it, and gave it to them and said: Take this, it is my body. And he took a cup, and when he had given thanks he gave it to them, and they all drank of it. And he said to them, This is my blood of the covenant, which is shed for many.

Verily I say to you, I shall not drink again of the fruit of the vine, until that day when I drink it new in the Kingdom of God. And when they had sung a hymn, they went out to the Mount of Olives.

MARK 14:22–26

THE LAST DAY

GETHSEMANE

JESUS SAID to the disciples, You will all leave me: for it is written, I will smite the shepherd and the sheep will be scattered. But after I am raised up, I will go before you to Galilee.

But Peter said to him, Even though they all leave you, yet I will not.

Jesus said to him, Verily I say to you, this very night, before the cock crows twice you will deny me thrice.

But he spoke the more vehemently, If I must die with you, I will not deny you. And they all said the same.

They came to a place called Gethsemane, and he said to his disciples, Sit here, while I pray. And he took with him Peter and James and John, and he began to be greatly distressed and troubled. And he said to them, My soul is very sorrowful, even to death. Stay here, and watch.

And he went forward a little, and fell on the ground, and prayed that if it were possible the hour might pass away from him. And he said, Abba, Father, all things are possible to thee; take this cup away from me. Yet not what I will, but what thou wilt.

And he came and found them sleeping and said to Peter, Simon, are you asleep? Could you not watch one hour? Watch and pray, that you may not enter into temptation. The spirit indeed is willing, but the flesh is weak.

And again he went away, and prayed, saying the same words. And again he came, and found them sleeping, for their eyes were very heavy, and they did not know what to answer him.

And he came the third time and said to them, Are you still sleeping, still taking your rest? It is enough; the hour has come. The Son of Man is betrayed into the hands of sinners. Rise up, let us go. Lo, he that betrays me is at hand.

MARK 14:27–42

BETRAYAL

WHILE HE was still speaking, Judas, one of the twelve, came with a crowd with swords and clubs, from the chief priests and scribes and elders, Now he that betrayed him had given them a sign, saying, Whoever I shall kiss, that is he. Seize him, and lead him away safely.

And as soon as he had come he went up to him and said, Rabbi, and kissed him.

And they laid their hands on him and seized him. But one of those that stood by drew his sword, and struck the servant of the high priest, and cut off his ear. And Jesus said to them, Have you come out as against a thief, to take me with swords and clubs? I was daily with you in the temple teaching, and you did not seize me. But let the scriptures be fulfilled. This is your hour and the power of darkness.

And they all forsook him and fled. And a young man followed him, with only a linen cloth about his body. And they laid hold of him, but he left the linen cloth and fled away naked.

MARK 14:43–52

THE TRIAL

THOSE WHO had seized Jesus led him to Caiaphas, the high priest, where the scribes and elders were assembled.

The high priest said to him, I adjure you by the living God, tell us whether you are the Christ, the Son of God.

Jesus said to him, You have said so. But I say to you, Hereafter you will see the Son of Man seated at the right hand of power, and coming on the clouds of heaven.

Then the high priest rent his robes, and said, He has spoken blasphemy, what further need have we of witnesses?

And when they had bound him, they led him away, and delivered him to Pilate, the governor.

MATTHEW 26:57,63–65; 27:2

THE GOVERNOR asked him, Are you the King of the Jews? Jesus replied, You have said so.

MATTHEW 27:11

JESUS SAID, My kingdom is not of this world: if my kingdom were of this world, then my servants would fight ... I came into the world to bear witness to the truth. Everyone who is of the truth hears my voice. Pilate said, What is truth?

When he had said this, he went out to the people again and said, I find no fault in him. They cried out, saying, If you let this man go, you are not Caesar's friend.

... Then he delivered him to them to be crucified.

JOHN 18:36 38; 19:12,16

AS THEY led him away, they laid hold of one Simon of Cyrene, who was coming in out of the country, and they laid the cross on him that he might bear it after Jesus. And there followed him a great company of people, and of women who bewailed and lamented him. But Jesus turned to them and said, Daughters of Jerusalem, do not weep for me, but weep for yourselves and for your children. For, behold, the days are coming in which they will say, Blessed are the barren, and the wombs that never bore, and the breasts that never gave suck. Then they will begin to say to the mountains, Fall on us; and to the hills, Cover us. For if they do these things in the green tree, what shall be done in the dry?

LUKE 23:26–31

THE CROSS

WHEN THEY came to a place called The Skull, there they crucified him, and two thieves, one on the right and the other on the left.

Then Jesus said, Father, forgive them, for they know not what they do. The people stood by watching, but the rulers derided him, saying, He saved others, let him save himself, if he is the Christ, the chosen of God.

The soldiers also mocked him, coming and offering him vinegar, and saying, If you are the King of the Jews, save yourself.

One of the thieves who were hanged taunted him, Are you not the Christ? Save yourself and us. But the other one rebuked him, saying, Do you not fear God, since you are in the same condemnation? We indeed justly, for we receive the due reward for our deeds. But this man has done nothing wrong. And he said, Jesus, remember me, when you come in your kingdom. Jesus said, Verily I say to you, today you will be with me in Paradise.

LUKE 23:33–43

WHEN MIDDAY had come, there was darkness over the whole land until three o'clock. And at three o'clock Jesus cried with a loud voice, *Eloi, Eloi, lama sabachthani*, which is, in translation, My God, my God, why hast thou forsaken me?

MARK 15:33–34

THEN JESUS cried with a loud voice, and said, Father, into thy hands I commit my spirit. And when he had said this he breathed his last.

LUKE 23:46

RESURRECTION FAITH

TOUCH ME NOT

O N THE first day of the week Mary Magdalene came to the sepulchre early, while it was still dark. She stood outside the sepulchre weeping. She turned herself back and saw Jesus standing, and did not know that it was Jesus.

Jesus said to her, Woman, why are you weeping? Who are you seeking?

Supposing him to be the gardener, she said to him, Sir, if you have removed him, tell me where you have laid him and I will take him away.

Jesus said to her, Mary.

She turned round and said to him, Rabboni (which means My Master).

Jesus said to her, Do not touch me; for I have not yet ascended to the Father. But go to my brothers and tell them that I am ascending to my Father, and your Father; to my God, and your God.

Mary Magdalene went and told the disciples, I have seen the Lord, and that he had said these things to her.

JOHN 20:1,14–18

THE ROAD TO EMMAUS

THAT SAME day two of them went to a village called Emmaus. And they talked together of all the things which had happened. And it came to pass, while they talked and discussed together, Jesus himself drew near and went with them, but their eyes were kept that they should not know him.

And he said to them, What are you talking about together as you walk? And they stood still, looking sad. And one of them, named Cleopas, answered, Are you the only one staying in Jerusalem who does not know the things that have happened there in these days? And he said, What things?

And they replied, Concerning Jesus of Nazareth, who was a prophet mighty in deed and word before God and all the people; and how the chief priests and our rulers sent him to be condemned to death, and crucified him. Yet we hoped that he was the one who would redeem Israel, but now it is the third day since all this happened.

Yet some women of our company astonished us; they went early to the sepulchre and did not find his body, but they came back saying that they had seen a vision of angels who said he was alive. Some of those who were with us went to the sepulchre and found it was as the women had said, but they did not see him.

Then he said to them, O foolish ones, and slow of heart to believe all that the prophets have spoken. Ought not Christ to have suffered these things, and enter into his glory? And beginning with Moses and all the prophets, he expounded in all the scriptures the things concerning himself.

And they drew near to the village to which they were going, and he made as though he would go farther. But they pleaded with him, saying, Stay with us, for it is towards evening, and the day is far spent. And he went in to stay with them.

And it came to pass, as he sat at table with them, he took the bread, and blessed and broke it, and gave it to them.

And their eyes were opened, and they knew him, and he vanished out of their sight. And they said to one another, Did not our hearts burn within us, while he talked with us on the way, and while he opened the scriptures to us? And they rose up that same hour, and returned to Jerusalem, and found the eleven gathered together, and those that were with them. And they told what had happened on the way, and how he was known to them in the breaking of the bread.

LUKE 24:13–35

WITH YOU ALWAYS

O N THE first day of the week, when the doors were shut where the disciples were, Jesus came and stood in the midst and said to them, Peace be with you. And when he had said this, he showed them his hands and his side. Then the disciples were glad when they saw the Lord.

Then Jesus said to them again, Peace be with you. As the Father sent me, so I am sending you. And when he had said this, he breathed on them and said, Receive the Holy Spirit. Whatever sins you forgive to any, they are forgiven; and whatever you retain of any, they are retained.

JOHN 20:19–23

T HE DISCIPLES asked him, Lord, will you at this time restore the kingdom to Israel? He replied, It is not for you to know the times or seasons which the Father has fixed by his own authority. But you will receive power, when the Holy Spirit has come upon you; and you shall be my witnesses in Jerusalem, and in all Judea, and to the ends of the earth.

ACTS 1:6–8

GO THEREFORE and make disciples of all nations, baptizing them in the name of the Father, and of the Son, and of the Holy Spirit; teaching them to observe all that I have commanded you. And lo, I shall be with you always, to the end of the age.

MATTHEW 28:19–20

THERE ARE also many other things which Jesus did which, if every one should be written, I suppose that the world itself could not contain the books that would be written.

JOHN 21:25

INDEX

ACKNOWLEDGEMENTS

The publisher would like to thank the following institutions for assistance and permission to produce the following pictures:

Robert Harding Picture Library (pp. 16, 41, 60, 73, 84, 104, 123, 148, 172, 164); The Hutchison Library (pp. 24, 29, 89, 161, 180, 209); Sonia Halliday Photographs (pp. 36, 109, 129, 168, 185, 216); The Art Archive (pp. 45, 113, 197, 220).